BORN-AGAIN POLITICS

The New Christian Right in America

Robert Zwier

InterVarsity Press
Downers Grove
Illinois 60515

InterVarsity Press is the book-publishing division of Inter-Varsity Christian Fellowship, a student movement active on campus at hundreds of universities, colleges and schools of nursing. For information about local and regional activities, write IVCF, 233 Langdon St., Madison, WI 53703.

Distributed in Canada through InterVarsity Press, 1875 Leslie St., Unit 10, Don Mills, Ontario M3B 2M5, Canada.

Bible quotations are from the Revised Standard Version, copyrighted 1946, 1952, © 1971, 1973, by the Division of Christian Education, National Council of the Churches of Christ in the USA, and used by permission.

Cover photograph: Jim Whitmer

ISBN 0-87784-828-9

Printed in the United States of America

Library of Congress Cataloging in Publication Data

Zwier, Robert, 1950-
    Born-again politics.

    Bibliography: p.
    1. Christianity and politics—History—20th
century.   2. Evangelicalism—United States—History
—20th century.   3. Fundamentalism—History—20th
century.   4. Conservatism—United States—History—
20th century.   5. United States—Politics and
government—1977-1981.   6. United States—Politics
and government-1981-   . I. Title.
BR115.P7Z94   1982   322'.1'0973   82-14006
ISBN 0-87784-828-9

18 17 16 15 14 13 12 11 10 9 8 7 6 5 4 3 2 1
95 94 93 92 91 90 89 88 87 86 85 84 83 82

1

Religion and Politics in the 1980s

EVERYONE IS AN EXPERT ON TWO subjects: religion and politics. Long hours of social conversation are devoted to roasting preachers and grilling politicians. Such discussions usually produce substantial heat but only faint light. Yet as the 1980 election drew near, the two topics were interwoven in a cloth so conspicuous that normally apathetic people cocked their ears and rubbed the political sleepers from their eyes.

The Christian Century magazine called it the biggest news story of the year.[1] Secular and religious periodicals raced to publish cover stories before the competition, and some religion editors of major newspapers could finally grab some front-page coverage. Here was a new toy in the play chest of political and religious journalism. Here was a crusade that pierced through the routine of once-a-Sunday worship serv-

ices and endless campaign speeches to artificially enthusiastic audiences. A handful of TV preachers, fundamentalist
in theology and conservative in politics, had teamed up with
a national hero of direct mail solicitation and several aggres-
sive right-wingers to heal this sickened nation, to instill
a moral sensitivity into a country filled with Watergates,
Korea-gates and Billy-gates, to restore trust and pride where
distrust and cynicism had reigned.

The New Christian Right, as it has come to be called, was
the strongest blend of religion and politics this country
had witnessed for decades. Surely, liberal theologians had
preached the evils of a war in far-off Vietnam and of race discrimination at home. But not in many years had preachers
so visibly and so vehemently proclaimed a message of political salvation that stretched over issues ranging from our
foreign policy toward tinhorn dictators to our domestic policy on day-care centers.

Now that the electoral dust has settled and the Republicans are setting the national agenda for budget cuts, now
that Norman Lear and George McGovern have sounded the
trumpet of opposition, now that social issues are creeping
toward the top of the congressional agenda, it is altogether
fitting to inquire about this politico-religious movement
called the New Christian Right. From its not-so-humble
beginnings on Sunday morning television to its triumphant
chorus of victories, this movement has changed the landscape of American politics: it has engendered hatred and
praise, fear and relief, anxiety and acclaim. Whether it be
a temporary fad or a bellwether of fundamental movement,
the New Christian Right has at least provoked our thoughts
and inspired our debates as this nation passes through the
Reagan revolution.

The New Christian Right
When we speak of the New Christian Right we are referring

to a loose coalition of groups grounded in religious fundamentalism and most visibly represented by Dr. Jerry Falwell with his Moral Majority, Incorporated, and by Rev. Robert Grant's California-based organization called Christian Voice. Simply to point to the fundamentalist roots will provoke controversy because the emphasis of the Moral Majority has recently taken a secular turn.

When the organization was first established in 1979 (chapter two will tell the story), the brochures and mailings were full of quotations from the Bible and references to God. For example, an early pamphlet said that the organization "was created to give a voice to the millions of decent, law-abiding, *God-fearing* Americans who want to do something about the moral decline of our country" (emphasis mine).[2] Another sentence in the same pamphlet uses the terms *Bible* and *morality* in such a way as to show vividly the religious orientation: "There are millions of Americans who love God, and decency, and Bible morality."[3]

Starting in the late summer of 1981, however, the organization began a media and mail campaign to identify itself as a moral rather than a religious organization. Interviewed by *Christianity Today*, Falwell insisted that "the Moral Majority is a *political* organization. You're not going to hear doctrine there. We are not going to try to witness to you there" (emphasis his).[4] In following chapters we will look more closely at this shift from a religious appeal to a moral appeal. Here it is enough to establish that the organization was conceived within a Christian community. Although much less visible than the Moral Majority, Christian Voice has expanded its membership, sought the victory of "moral" candidates or the defeat of "immoral" ones, and pushed hard to achieve legislation eliminating the social sins of American society.

The primary audience, or constituency, for these groups was the approximately 50 million evangelicals in the country and in particular the fundamentalist wing of this community. The aim from the beginning was to mobilize a group of people who had traditionally avoided politics because they saw it as a dirty, corrupt business in their rather Manichean view of good and evil. By convincing these people that political involvement was a God-given responsibility, the New Christian Right repeated the rhetoric of the 1950s when Carl McIntire and others called for a similar awakening among Protestant fundamentalists.

Like these earlier movements, the contemporary Christian Right sought allies within the traditionally active political sector. Beginning at least with the Carter victory in 1976, due in some small part at least to evangelical voting, several secular conservative figures such as Richard Viguerie, Gary Jarmin and Paul Weyrich dreamed dreams of capturing this enormous block of potential voters. Coalescing under the loose auspices of the National Conservative Political Action Committee, these political movers made overtures to Falwell and others to combine forces in the quest to control the White House. Their eyes were clearly focused on a Reagan candidacy because of the strength the Californian had shown in nearly taking the Republican nomination away from an incumbent president in 1976. While the liberal drift of the Carter administration reduced their already weak support for the Baptist from Georgia, these spokesmen renewed their commitment to make the 1980 election a watershed in American politics.

The 1980 Election
Thus it was with whetted appetites that the Vigueries, Jarmins and Weyrichs noted the politization of the electronic church. Viguerie, already an acknowledged master of mass mailings, had high respect for the ability of Falwell's "Old Time Gospel Hour" to pull in millions of dollars each year. An alliance between the conservatives and the TV preacher

was established, and with the Reagan nomination in Detroit the 1980 campaign was launched.

It was an intense campaign, and intensely difficult for evangelical voters. Not only did the home-town Sunday-school teacher from Plains win the Democratic nomination, but another candidate staked a claim to the evangelical constituency that was to figure so significantly in the Reagan strategy. Congressman John Anderson from Illinois had for many years explained votes on the basis of his Christian beliefs, spoken at Christian college commencements and participated in prayer breakfasts and Bible studies on Capitol Hill. So the three major candidates were ready and willing to battle for the votes of a waking evangelical community.

Although Anderson suffered from the legal, political and financial difficulties faced by all minor party candidates in U.S. national elections, there was the possibility that he might win enough Electoral College votes so that the Democratic-controlled House of Representatives would ultimately decide who would be president in the first half of what Falwell calls the "Decade of Destiny." Such a scenario haunted the New Christian Right and increased its determination to persuade the men and women of the pews. Throughout the contest, public opinion polls reported only marginal advantages and, more importantly, large numbers of undecided and volatile voters. Newspapers and magazines around the country began to take note of the New Christian Right and the publicity served for a while to reinforce its incipient significance.

It was not really until the middle of the campaign that religious and political liberals realized what was happening and began to counterattack. Arguments about the biblical positions on the Panama Canal treaty or SALT II flew furiously across the printed page. Liberal pastors took to their pulpits to denounce the intolerance of the Moral Majority and Christian Voice, while their professional colleagues down the street proclaimed the biblical truths of political conservatism. Not in many years had congregations experienced such intense pulpit politicking. For many fundamentalists the last time had been in 1960 when the nation faced the imminent prospect of a hotline between the Oval Office and the Vatican.

In the closing weeks of the campaign as the debates reached new heights of righteousness, many candidates felt themselves losing control of their own campaigns. Some of those for whom the New Christian Right were campaigning noticed the increasingly strident language and saw some moderate votes slipping away—not because of something they or their opponents were doing but because of the way citizens were reacting to the religious appeals. Several candidates attempted to put some distance between themselves and the new Christian groups; the last thing they wanted was to become involved in a debate about the proper biblical perspective on legislation they might encounter.

As election day dawned, the polls showed a slight edge for Reagan and some indications that Republican congressional candidates might erode some of the comfortable Democratic majority in Congress. But in addition to these questions about individual victories or defeats was the significant question of the extent to which the evangelical vote would signal the conversion of American politics.

It did not take long to answer the first set of questions. Even before the polls closed in Western states, President Carter had conceded defeat, and the only question left was the margin of victory. It turned out to be overwhelming, particularly in Electoral College votes. As if that were not enough, the voting patterns began to show signs of a large congressional victory for Republicans. When the last vote had been counted, the Republicans sat atop a 53-seat majority in the Senate and had whittled 49 seats from the Democratic majority in the House.

At the center of the revolution in the Senate was the defeat of senior, liberal Democrats such as Frank Church of Idaho, John Culver of Iowa, George McGovern of South Dakota, Gaylord Nelson of Wisconsin and Birch Bayh of Indiana. These men had been the target of the attack by none other than the New Christian Right. Although the religious groups had also wanted to evict Alan Cranston from his California seat, their efforts in that state had been relatively minimal. Where they had pulled out all the stops, their senatorial candidates had won. So the second question—the question about evangelical voting power—loomed large over the landscape newly littered with defeated liberals. The New Christian Right quickly claimed a great victory and within days presented a hit list for the 1982 elections. Leaders of the National Conservative Political Action Committee gleefully accepted postelection interviews so they could announce the transformation of American society. While Ronald Reagan more soberly pondered the assumption of the most powerful office on earth, scholars, journalists, and preachers looked over the vote patterns to measure the effects of the evangelical renaissance.

The 1980 election brought into sharp focus the two topics of this book: religion and politics. This watershed contest raised again the questions about the proper role of Christians in the political process and about the rights of interest groups to fashion society in their own images. As we move through this Decade of Destiny, it is appropriate to examine the role of the New Christian Right in the campaign and to speculate about its future as a significant political force in our governing system. In addition, it is appropriate to raise more abstract questions about the proper blend of religion and politics in a democracy and in a pluralistic society.

The Roadmap
This book is about the latest mix of fundamentalist religion

and conservative politics. It is neither an apologetic for nor a denunciation of the New Christian Right, although one aim is to look at the arguments of the groups' supporters and detractors. It is rather a book concerned with understanding: understanding why this brew of religion and politics boiled over in 1980, understanding what the New Christian Right seeks to do to and for this nation, and understanding whether their evangelical constituency will follow where they lead.

Chapter two examines the roots of the New Christian Right. In particular, we will observe the triggering events of the 1970s which led Falwell, Grant and others to form political movements; we will survey the organizations they created; and we will trace the concurrent flowering of the secular new right and their finding religion.

Chapter three focuses on the platform of the new movement by considering the underlying biblical and political assumptions on which it rests and by showing how these assumptions lead to specific issue positions that make conservative ideologues proud. Of special importance in this chapter are the differences within the New Christian Right; despite the fact that several observers have lumped them all into one undifferentiated mass, some positions are held by one group but not by others. It is important in our understanding to make these distinctions.

In chapter four we will look more closely at the New Christian Right as a set of interest groups. Political scientists have provided insights and concepts that will help us to understand the organization and strategies of groups like the Moral Majority and Christian Voice. Not only will we examine such campaign tactics as legislative report cards, but we will also investigate the crucial factors of grassroots organizing and fund raising.

Chapter five will assess the role of the New Christian Right in the 1980 elections, with particular emphasis on the senatorial election in Iowa. This election was the first test of strength of the new movement, and each group spent hundreds of thousands of dollars to ensure the defeat of "immoral" candidates. We must see whether the conservative success in 1980 resulted specifically from the efforts of the New Christian Right, or whether the groups were carried along on a wave of conservative sentiment that they did not create.

In chapter six we will examine the support for the New Christian Right among evangelical pastors. Relying on a mail questionnaire sent to ministers in Iowa and South Dakota, we will assess whether the New Christian Right strategy of depending on ministers to mobilize their congregations is likely to be successful.

The focus of chapter seven is the reaction of the broader Christian community to the platform and tactics of the movement. We will study the often intense arguments of those who see these groups as the worst examples of religious intolerance and biblical selectiveness. On the other hand, we will notice the relief among some evangelicals that at last someone is showing concern about the immorality of our society.

Chapter eight looks to the future to see the short- and long-term future of the New Christian Right as it seeks to elect moral candidates and design legislation that will restore this country to moral health. The final section of the chapter will offer some reflections about the broader questions of mixing religion and politics, offering some advice to Christians who seek to promote their biblical perspectives in the political realm and to non-Christians who must live with this righteous army of zealots. There is an inherent conflict between strong religious convictions and societal pluralism; we must see whether there is any possibility of peaceful coexistence.

As we proceed on this journey, we should remember that the names and faces are new but that questions about the union of religion and politics are seemingly eternal. In every age concerns about the proper blending of the cross and the flag confront preachers, politicians and citizens as they seek to create a society which reflects the broader vision and higher principles which they hold. All too often advocates of one sort or another try to argue for the predominance of either the cross or the flag without realizing the useful symbiosis that has developed over time. Religious convictions have brought to politics a necessary sense of right and wrong; politics has brought to religion a recognition of the importance of this world and its patterns of justice. The emergence of the New Christian Right encourages us to reflect again on these things.

2
The Roots of the New Christian Right

WITHIN THE NEW CHRISTIAN RIGHT movement the largest and most visible group is Falwell's Moral Majority. This group has been receiving the most attention from the media, from the religious community and from the general public, if bumper stickers are any indication. Another group which has been more explicitly religious in its appeals is Christian Voice; its greatest claim to fame was the publication in 1980 of a legislative report card which evaluated the votes of members of Congress on fourteen bills and resolutions. The activities of these two groups are the focus of this study, and so it is well at the outset to look at the groups themselves, their leaders and their roots in the political events of the 1970s.

The Groups and Their Leaders
The Moral Majority, like Christian Voice, is a product of

the discontent among fundamentalist preachers as they examined the general drift of public policy and societal norms in the 1970s. The founder and president of the organization is Jerry Falwell, pastor of the 17,000-member Thomas Road Baptist Church of Lynchburg, Virginia, and preacher to many more through his weekly TV broadcast, "The Old Time Gospel Hour."

Born in 1933, Falwell was mightily influenced by the alcohol-related death of his father, for this experience convinced him of the importance of personal lifestyle issues. In school he was an average student. Upon graduation from high school (which he missed because of a punishment for one of his constant pranks), he enrolled in the mechanical engineering program at Lynchburg College. Not a regular churchgoer, in January 1952 he attended services at the Park Avenue Baptist Church and was moved to conversion. Falwell decided to go into the ministry, and he registered at Bible Baptist College in Springfield, Missouri. With his degree in hand he returned to Lynchburg and founded the Thomas Road Church, starting with only a handful of adults.

From that point on, nearly everything he touched has been successful. Falwell started Liberty Baptist College in 1971, later adding a seminary and a Christian day school. His "Old Time Gospel Hour" is now broadcast on almost 400 stations and in 1980 took in over $50 million. This phenomenal success, however, left Falwell unsatisfied because of what he saw in the society around him. Concerned with the decline in morality and with government decisions about abortion, private schools, gambling and women's liberation, Falwell sought to create an organization that would address these political and social problems.

In June 1979 he and Robert Billings set up the Moral Majority. It too has experienced rapid growth, reaching a membership of 4 to 5 million people (although not all of them are contributing or active members). Included in this group are nearly 75,000 pastors, priests and rabbis. There are Moral Majority affiliates in all 50 states and in the District of Columbia. In some states the group is organized down to the county level. Nearly every state organization is led by a minister, in most cases a Baptist. The group's newsletter, *Moral Majority Report*, is sent to almost 1 million homes, and a radio broadcast by the same name is heard over 300 stations. The Moral Majority budget surpasses $5.5 million per year, with the bulk of the money spent on lobbying and publications.

Although Robert Billings has left the organization to join the Reagan administration, the leadership has been quite stable. The board of directors includes Falwell, Charles Stanley (First Baptist Church of Atlanta), Greg Dixon (Indianapolis Baptist Temple), Tim LaHaye (Christian Heritage College) and James Kennedy (Coral Ridge Presbyterian Church of Fort Lauderdale). The organization's vice president is Dr. Ronald Godwin, who was an administrator at two Christian colleges before joining Falwell. The Moral Majority has a Washington lobbying staff of about a half-dozen people, although none of them has had much legislative or lobbying experience.

The group also established a Moral Majority political action committee in 1980 which was supposed to make contributions and endorse candidates. However, the committee was not able to raise as much money as they had hoped, and leaders feared that the little money they were raising was hurting the fund raising of the parent organization; so the political action committee was given only secondary priority. Another offspring, the Moral Majority Legal Defense Foundation, has been more successful. This group seeks to provide legal assistance to various causes, especially private schools and those who are battling pornography, drugs and homosexuality at the local level.

Although we will examine the Moral Majority political platform in much greater detail in the next chapter, we should

note at this point the primary goals of the organization. Their
early literature suggests the following objectives:
   1. to mobilize moral Americans into a loud political voice;
   2. to inform moral Americans about government policies;
   3. to lobby in Congress in order to defeat liberal bills;
   4. to push for positive legislation that would insure a free
America; and
   5. to aid citizens who are waging political battles in their
home towns.
   On the other side of the country, Rev. Robert Grant established Christian Voice in 1978. Despite the geographic distance from Lynchburg to Pasadena, the objectives of the two
groups are very similar. Grant's organization, like Falwell's,
was set up by a group of ministers who had been active in several local and state campaigns against homosexuality. Robert
Grant, like Falwell, is unusually energetic and amiable.
Educated at St. Paul (Minnesota) Bible College, Wheaton
College, Fuller Theological Seminary and the California
Graduate School of Theology, Grant has long sought to bring
the standards of the Bible to bear on current social issues.
As one of the founders of American Christian Cause, he has
been active in dealing with homosexuals, helping Anita
Bryant in her Florida campaign as well as participating in
several California battles. In addition to this political activity, Grant served for a time as dean of the California Graduate School of Theology, and he still serves as a travel agent
specializing in religious tours.
   Christian Voice too has grown, although not nearly so
quickly as the Moral Majority. Christian Voice has about
400,000 members (again, not all are contributing and active)
drawn from several denominations. The group focuses on
recruiting the clergy who, it is hoped, will work to mobilize
their own congregations. Special mailings go to clergy to
alert them to important legislative battles; through these
mailings the group seeks to generate a flood of letters from

constituents to their congressional representatives as key votes approach. Christian Voice, unlike the Moral Majority, does not have official state chapters, but contact persons are in every state and some states do have informal but active working groups. The initially high budget expectations have not been achieved; the group has been operating on a budget of approximately $1 million per year.

Christian Voice does have a more active political action committee than the Moral Majority. The Christian Voice Moral Government Fund endorsed the candidacy of Ronald Reagan and spent about $400,000 in independent efforts to defeat liberal incumbents in such targeted states as Iowa, South Dakota and California. As we will see in chapter five, many of the candidates they targeted for defeat did in fact lose, although it is doubtful that the Christian Voice activity was the primary cause. In the 1982 elections the Moral Government Fund was again active in carefully selected states where liberal incumbents were thought to be the most vulnerable. The organization also has a small lobbying team in Washington, D.C., headed by Gary Jarmin. Jarmin, an experienced lobbyist, is one of the ties between the New Christian Right and other conservative groups. He was formerly an official of the Rev. Sun Myung Moon's Unification Church and a lobbyist for the American Conservative Union.

The executive board has experienced much turnover, but among the people who have served at various times are Grant, Hal Lindsey (*The Late, Great Planet Earth*), Ted Hurlburt (pastor), Jess Moody (pastor), Donald Sills (pastor), Robert Morgan (attorney) and Paul Webb (Los Angeles TV producer). In addition to this group, Christian Voice also has a national advisory board composed of people from all walks of life. The exact division of responsibilities among these groups is not clear, but having both groups certainly provides more opportunities for group supporters to have some measure of involvement in the group's efforts. The organization also relies on an advisory board composed of conservative members of Congress. Among its members are Senators Jepsen, Hatch and McClure, as well as Congressmen Ashbrook, Crane and McDonald. There has been some turnover here too. Some members of the advisory committee resigned when the Christian Voice legislative report card was issued because they did not want to be associated with an effort that implied the immorality of congressional colleagues.

While the Moral Majority has modified the basis of its appeal from religion to morality, Christian Voice has consistently sought support from evangelicals and has argued for its policy positions on the basis of its interpretation of Scripture. The initial Statement of Purpose and several subsequent letters make clear the centrality of their religious convictions. For example, the Statement of Purpose announces that "Christian Voice seeks to restore moral accountability to American life, to re-focus the eyes of her leaders and her people on God, and to turn the tide of battle against Satan's forces." Furthermore, the document claims, "We believe that 'righteousness exalts a nation' and we seek God's guidance and blessing in all endeavors, trusting He intends us to be victorious."

The Roots
Politics in America has witnessed other religious groups seeking political influence, and some of these have even made the same appeals to moralism and patriotism that we find with the New Christian Right. Yet the movement that encompasses the Moral Majority and Christian Voice is a unique consummation of several trends and events that highlighted the decade of the 1970s. To understand these two groups, we must look briefly at their short history and particularly their emergence from important political and religious events since 1970. Our examination of these roots

will be divided into two sections: the first will analyze the most important trigger events of the decade, and the second will present the broader facilitating events that allowed and encouraged Falwell and Grant to establish these two groups.

Trigger events. The New Christian Right was born out of the battles which fundamentalist Christians waged and, for the most part, lost in the 1970s. Four events in particular provoked the right-wing Christian community into action; these were the 1973 Supreme Court decision on abortion, the gay rights movement, the proposal by the Internal Revenue Service to question the tax-exempt status of some private schools and the proposed Equal Rights Amendment.

One of the foremost causes of both Christian Voice and the Moral Majority is abortion. Thoroughly upset that 1.5 million abortions would be performed in a single year and frustrated that many Christians were not up in arms about the trend toward easier abortions, Falwell and Grant established groups that would work with other prolife groups to enact restrictions on what they saw as 1.5 million murders each year.

The 1973 decision by the U.S. Supreme Court in the case *Roe v. Wade* set the stage for this moral struggle. The case involved a young, single Texas woman (Jane Roe) who sought to obtain an abortion but was prevented by a Texas law that made abortions a crime unless the mother's life was threatened. Roe's counsel argued before the Court that the central issue was the right to privacy: Jane Roe had a right which could not constitutionally be restricted by government. The right in this case involved a decision to terminate her pregnancy. In a 7-2 decision the court ruled in her favor, but the opinion clearly stated that the right to have an abortion is not an absolute right.

A brief look at the decision will help us to understand the harsh reaction among both Catholics and Protestants. First, the Court decided that the right to privacy "is broad enough to encompass a woman's decision whether or not to terminate her pregnancy."[1] The Court agreed that carrying and bearing an unwanted child could result in mental or physical harm to either the mother or the child. But faced with the argument that such a right was absolute, the Court disagreed: the decisions "recognizing a right of privacy also acknowledge that some state regulation in areas protected by that right is appropriate. A state may properly assert important interests in safeguarding health, in maintaining medical standards, and in protecting potential life." The court was much less clear on the matter of which state regulations were appropriate and, in particular, when they were permissible.

Briefly reviewing the controversy about when life begins, the justices argued against the idea that personhood, as protected by the Fourteenth Amendment, begins at the moment of conception. Instead they divided up the period of pregnancy into three trimesters. Fundamentalists were particularly incensed by the opinion that during the first trimester the state may not impose any restrictions on the woman's right to have an abortion. A woman, in consultation with her physician, may simply decide to obtain one. During the second trimester, the state may enact some guidelines focusing on the health of the mother. For example, the state could regulate who could perform abortions, where they could be done and the like. Nothing at this point conveys any awareness of the fetus. At the end of the sixth month, the point of viability according to the Court, the state may become concerned with the child and may prohibit abortions except to preserve the life and health of the mother. The Court did not require states to prohibit abortions in the last trimester, but it did allow them to do so.

For a group of Christians who argue that human life begins at the moment of conception, this decision was a disaster. Each year the anniversary of the decision is marked by protests, picketing and renewed attempts to petition the Congress and the president to overrule this decision. The New Christian Right was aided greatly in its initial months by the organizing that prolife groups have been doing since 1973. In other words, the right-to-life movement laid a solid institutional framework and conducted the initial mobilization that the Moral Majority and Christian Voice could capture for their broader political vision. Had these people not already been activated, the New Christian Right could not have had any significant impact in the 1980 elections.

The other three trigger events related more directly and closely to the formation of the groups. Christian Voice, in particular, resulted from the battle over homosexual rights in California. In 1978 a ballot proposition in that state would have expanded the legal protection of homosexuals. A group of fundamentalist pastors, including Robert Grant, became involved in a campaign to defeat the measure. At one point the Internal Revenue Service warned these pastors about the tax-exempt status of their churches in the light of their political activities. Unwilling to stop the fight, but hesitant to damage their churches, the ministers formed Christian Voice as a political organization. Through this instrument the individuals could achieve their political objectives without worrying about their churches.

A second event instrumental in the formation of both groups was another Internal Revenue Service action, this one dealing with the tax-exempt status of private schools. The number of these schools had risen rapidly since the Court's 1954 desegregation decision in *Brown* v. *Board of Education, Topeka, Kansas*. It was clear to many observers that some of these new schools were established to avoid the desegregation that the Court mandated for public schools. Thus many of these schools were called "white flight" schools.

IRS Commissioner Jerome Kurtz, in response to demands from Blacks and other groups, developed a proposal that could have denied the tax-exempt status of some of these private schools. Specifically the IRS labeled as "reviewable" any tax exemption for a school that had been created in a district under a desegregation ruling. For these reviewable schools the IRS established a guideline to measure discrimination. A school could retain its tax status if it enrolled five per cent of the proportion of minorities living in the area. For example, if minorities comprised ten per cent of an area, then a school would have to have a two per cent minority enrollment. If a school failed that test, it could still maintain its status by demonstrating that it was making a good-faith effort to hire minority teachers and to recruit minority students.

These proposals triggered storms of protest among fundamentalists, many of whom support religious schools. To them it looked as if the IRS were simply presuming guilt for any school created after 1954. Some Christian groups generated a letter-writing campaign and deluged IRS offices with over 120,000 letters—apparently an IRS record. In response, the IRS held an emotional four-day hearing and backed off. Not yet satisfied, the private-school supporters asked Congress to act, and within a year Congress had approved a measure cutting off funds for implementation of the IRS proposal. This battle was especially crucial for Falwell, who was a leader in the private-school movement in Virginia; and Grant called it an important catalyst in the formation of Christian Voice. What it demonstrated above all was that the government would respond to a mass protest and that such a protest could be stimulated through the mass mailing techniques and clergy appeals they were increasingly employing.

Finally, the battle over the Equal Rights Amendment to the Constitution was a trigger event, particularly for Falwell who was an important influence in the decision of the Virginia legislature to reject the ratification of the amendment.

Although Falwell subsequently admitted that he would support an equal rights amendment that specifically prohibited homosexual marriages and adoptions and would forbid drafting women into the armed services, he and others were dissatisfied with the precise wording of the amendment which had passed the Congress. He claimed that the wording was too vague and that there was too much danger that the courts would outlaw all distinctions between men and women. Such a position, he argued, was contrary to biblical teachings about the proper roles of men and women.

Again we have an instance of other groups beginning a fight which the Moral Majority later joined. The New Christian Right was able to capitalize on the organizational work already accomplished, especially in this case at the state level where the battle was being fought. As was the case with abortion, the most fertile soil for opponents of the ERA was the fundamentalist community with their claims to scriptural clarity and applicability. The opportunity was not wasted; the Moral Majority cooperated with other anti-ERA groups to defeat the amendment in various state legislatures and to threaten legislators who voted the wrong way.

These four events were the most important reasons for the birth of the New Christian Right. By provoking groups of concerned citizens, the government had ignited a spark that would burn for several years on conservative and religious altars. In addition, several other events were important for setting up the context in which the New Christian Right could operate. To understand the origins and the current strength of the Moral Majority and Christian Voice, we must look briefly at these roots.

Facilitators.   Perhaps the most important facilitator during the late 1970s was the concurrent rise of what has been called the secular new right. Included in this group are such people as Richard Viguerie (mass mailing expert), Paul Weyrich (leader of a group called the Committee for the Survival of a Free Congress), Howard Phillips (head of the Conservative Caucus) and Terry Dolan (leader of the National Conservative Political Action Committee). These four men and the groups they represent played a very important part in convincing Jerry Falwell to form a political organization, and they had a crucial role to play in the Reagan campaign in 1980.

The secular new right had its own roots back in the presidential elections of 1960 and 1964. Prior to these elections, the South had been solidly Democratic even though many of the elected officials were as conservative in ideology as some Republicans. The increasingly liberal trend within the Democratic Party, signified by the nomination of John Kennedy and the party's support for the civil-rights cause, produced among some southern conservatives a negative reaction, leading them to vote for Nixon in 1960 and Goldwater in 1964. This trend away from the Democrats continued in 1968 with the candidacy of George Wallace on the American Independent Party ticket. By the late 1960s Kevin Phillips was predicting a significant increase in support for the Republican Party from these disaffected southerners.[2]

This movement provided a ray of hope for Republicans who had seen their popular support dwindle since Roosevelt's New Deal coalition and who had seen solid Democratic majorities in Congress since the middle 1950s. The likelihood that Republican candidates would be competitive in presidential elections led conservative Republicans to renew their efforts to make sure that the party nominated a conservative.

Consequently, the four men mentioned above set up their groups in the late 1960s and early 1970s. In their quest for supporters they began to look at the voting patterns of evangelicals and were delighted to find a preference for conservative candidates. The problem they faced was that many of these citizens were not very active politically; the strategy then was to mobilize this block of people, which they estimated to include between 30 and 50 million potential voters. In their occasional joint strategy sessions, the groups focused on the best means to activate the evangelicals and decided that some of the television preachers like Falwell had the most influence over these people.

As early as 1976 some of the new right leaders were talking to Falwell and others involved in the electronic church. The big push, however, came in 1978 as the new right sought the defeat of several liberal legislators and formed an alliance with groups against abortion and the Equal Rights Amendment. At the same time Weyrich met again with Falwell and convinced him to set up his own political group. Whether the Moral Majority would have been set up without this encouragement is unclear; what is certain is that these appeals showed Falwell that key people with the political skills he lacked were ready to stand by him in his new political role. As this alliance between a crucial segment of the Republican Party and a popular leader of the Christian community blossomed in the late 1970s, it represented a significant threat to liberal office holders and candidates.

A second facilitator was the person and the presidency of Jimmy Carter. His campaign for national office in 1976 first demonstrated the possibility of mobilizing evangelicals. By wearing proudly the label of a deeply religious man, Carter was able to attract voters who were looking for an end to the era of Watergate and corruption at the highest levels of government. Candidate Carter drew attention to his religious convictions and argued that these beliefs would influence his behavior in the Oval Office. Certainly a Sunday-school teacher from Plains could be trusted to act morally in office.

When the national media finally turned their attention to Carter, the focus was on the born-again Christian. When the votes were counted and analyzed, it was clear that Carter had captured strong evangelical support. What was especially significant about the Carter presidency for many future supporters of the New Christian Right was that he deemed it perfectly legitimate for a born-again Christian to become deeply involved in politics. This openness to political activity set the stage for the Moral Majority and Christian Voice. While these two groups grew disenchanted with Carter's presidency, they were able to use his religiosity for their own purposes. They were able to argue that religious convictions do affect political decisions and that Christians are able to become involved in politics without losing their souls to the devil.

A third phenomenon facilitating the emergence of the Moral Majority in particular was the increasing visibility of the television church.[3] The airwaves on Sunday mornings (and increasingly at other times) were filled with preachers proclaiming a message of salvation and denouncing the sins of American society. Without the weekly audience of Falwell's "Old Time Gospel Hour," it is unlikely that the Moral Majority would have grown so rapidly in its first two years. Millions of Americans had watched this smooth and sincere preacher, responding to his appeals with millions of dollars in contributions. It seemed legitimate for these viewers then to support Falwell's new political organization.

The increasing importance of cable television too has helped the New Christian Right. By encouraging the development of a distinctly Christian network, cable television opened up a convenient instrument that could be used effectively by the preacher-politician activists. Both Christian Voice and the Moral Majority claim to have a standing invitation to appear on such popular programs as "The 700 Club" and "PTL." A receptive audience of trusting, Bible-believing Christians awaits their appeals for support, money and action. To be sure, Falwell makes a sincere effort to separate his leadership of the Moral Majority from his weekly broadcast, but in the minds of many viewers—and also many in the national news media—the boundary is blurred. Media stories about his Moral Majority activities almost inevitably mention "The Old Time Gospel Hour," and several themes raised on the weekly TV program are identical to the concerns of his interest group.

Another important event which laid a foundation for the New Christian Right was the passage in 1974 of a law regulating the financing of election campaigns. At first glance the connection between the campaign finance act and the New Christian Right seems remote, but the linkage can be made. What the law did was to put a ceiling on the amount of money any individual could contribute to a campaign. The limit was $1000 per election (the primary election and the general election count separately), with an overall ceiling for each individual of $25,000 per year. What may be even more important is the provision that a political action committee could contribute up to $5000 per election with no overall limit.

These two provisions led to a rapid increase in the number of political action committees, such as the Christian Voice Moral Government Fund. Another provision in the act established a system of public financing for presidential elections. This money would only go to those candidates who could first raise small amounts of money in several different states. The money which the candidate could use to qualify for federal funding had to be raised with contributions of $250 or less. The practical effect of these provisions was that candidates could no longer rely on just a few large contributors; they would now have to seek much smaller amounts from many more people.

In terms of tactics, the best way to raise this money was through direct mailings. In the middle 1970s, therefore, a whole new industry sprang to life offering mailing lists and facilities to potential candidates. At the head of this new industry was Richard Viguerie, who had set up shop back in 1965; he was inundated with requests following the passage of the 1974 law. He had started the Richard A. Viguerie Company in 1965 with about 12,000 names and has since expanded his mailing list to more than 4 million.

When the secular new right approached Falwell in late 1978, they could assure him of access to their huge list of possible supporters. This offer proved irresistible, especially because Falwell had been working on expanding his own mailing list from "The Old Time Gospel Hour." The prospect of an alliance between the leading political mass mailer and one of the leading religious mass mailers certainly whetted appetites on both sides and opened the door to further discussions. By convincing these two men of the importance of their mailing skills, the 1974 campaign finance act facilitated the efforts to set up the Moral Majority as a citizens interest group and encouraged Christian Voice to set up its Moral Government Fund.

Another facilitating event, which was more distant in terms of time but which evoked considerable concern among the New Christian Right, was a pair of Supreme Court decisions in the early 1960s. In the case of *Engel* v. *Vitale* (1962) the Court ruled that a nondenominational prayer prepared for school use by the New York Board of Regents was in violation of the First Amendment clause prohibiting the government from establishing a religion.[4] One year later, in the case of *Abington School District* v. *Schempp*, the Court claimed that the First Amendment establishment clause prohibited public school practices "requiring the selection and reading at the opening of the school day of verses from the Holy Bible and the recitation of the Lord's Prayer by the students in unison."[5] Even though the Pennsylvania law challenged in this case provided for students to be excused from the practice upon the request of parents, the Court decided that the practice was more than the Constitution allowed.

These two decisions provoked an intense reaction in many school districts and aided in the growth of the private school phenomenon we have already noted. For both Christian Voice and the Moral Majority, kicking God out of the public schools was an important step in the ascendancy of the philosophy of secular humanism which lay at the root of many societal ills in the 1970s.[6] Viewing these two decisions alongside the 1973 abortion decision, we can understand why the New Christian Right is sympathetic to appeals to restrict the jurisdiction or power of the Supreme Court, why it is hesitant to accept the vague wording of the Equal Rights Amendment and why it is concerned about the Reagan nominations to the Supreme Court.

Finally, earlier political efforts within the fundamentalist community helped to provide an audience for the appeals of Falwell, Grant and others. Although the connection between people like Carl McIntire and Jerry Falwell is probably indirect at best, from the perspective of the common constituency it is important to understand something about the earlier movement.

The emergence of twentieth-century fundamentalism is best related by George Marsden.[7] Although Marsden argues that the fundamentalism of the 1920s was not primarily a political movement, it did have ties to the anticommunist fever running through the decade. Of more direct significance was the decade of the 1950s and the efforts among fundamentalists to denounce the mainline Protestant churches, to renew the attack on the communists (with the help of Senator McCarthy) and to preserve the purity of doctrine within the churches and seminaries. The key figures in this struggle were Carl McIntire, Billy James Hargis, Edgar Bundy and Fred Schwartz.[8]

Expounding a doctrine of religious patriotism, these lead-

ers and the groups they established directed their appeals
to the Protestant fundamentalists (or as Clabaugh calls them,
the Fundradists) who were concerned about communism,
liberalism and heresy. These men also had direct ties to the
extreme right wing of the Republican Party as well as to the
John Birch Society. Following the best tradition of conspiracy theories, many of them claimed that the United States
was under assault from the international communist movement, of which American liberalism, worldwide ecumenical
movements and the welfare state mentality were all a part.
Preaching their gospel of political religion, they were active
in the Goldwater campaign; his overwhelming defeat took
much of the wind from their sails.

The link to the New Christian Right appeals is best seen
in Gary Clabaugh's description of the 1960s movement:
"[They] drape themselves in the robes of Jesus Christ while
fanatically waving the American flag."[9] Many of the appeals
are the same, and the audience is largely the same. What
distinguishes the New Christian Right from the Fundradists
is the willingness of the more recent groups to include Jews,
Catholics, Mormons and Blacks in their midst, reflecting
an attitude of greater tolerance than McIntire ever demonstrated. Although contemporary critics of the New Christian
Right see the movement as dangerously intolerant, by historical perspective the new groups are much more open to
a wider range of people.

Summary
The purpose of this chapter has been to outline the structure
of the two groups that are in the forefront of the New Christian Right and to trace in some detail their roots in the history of the postwar period. As we have seen, both Christian
Voice and the Moral Majority are large groups with fairly
complex organizational structures. At the helm are men
who have been politically active in state campaigns against

homosexuality, women's liberation and government involvement in private schools. Although both groups claim to be ecumenical, it is apparent that the bulk of their supporters are Protestant fundamentalists and that at least a plurality of the key leadership is Baptist. The groups were formed in the late 1970s as reactions to events such as the IRS moves against Christian schools, Supreme Court decisions concerning abortion and religion in the public schools, and the expansion of the civil-rights movement to women and homosexuals. Their ties to a group of young, energetic Republicans foretell an active political role in the Decade of Destiny. As long as the government is controlled by liberals, there will be a common enemy which will work to unite these organizations.

3
The Political Platform of the New Christian Right

THE NEW CHRISTIAN RIGHT WANTS to turn the United States around. It wants to restore this nation to the biblical morality that it claims was the guiding light for our founding fathers. Such a conversion requires an internally consistent, intensely pursued program of political, economic and social reforms that would make any ideological conservative turn numerous shades of proud.

The platform of the New Christian Right, while not totally congruent with that of the Republican Party in 1980, reflects similar assumptions and calls for many of the same programs. This is not surprising. As we have seen, the groups associated with the New Christian Right supported the candidacy of Ronald Reagan, who was responsible for the formulation of large parts of the Republican platform. In an interview with *Christianity Today,* Falwell could barely conceal his absolute delight at the Reagan presidency: "I do think that Mr. Reagan is the greatest thing that has happened to our country in my lifetime."[1] This statement certainly represents a bit of both hyperbole and historical myopia, yet through it shines the glimmers of optimism as the movement anticipated the Reagan agenda.

Our understanding of the movement will be complete only if we study carefully its call to action. Clearly, the groups were founded at just the right time in American history. These religious-political organizations were able to take advantage of the national dissatisfaction with the policy failures of the Great Society liberals and the consequent urge to try something different. The major purposes of this chapter are to examine the underlying assumptions or presuppositions of the New Christian Right, to look at the specific issue positions that flow from it and to make the necessary distinctions among the people and groups associated with the movement. Not every group has taken a position on each issue, so we must be careful to attribute to the Moral Majority, for example, only what they have claimed. In order to do this, we will depend heavily on official documents, brochures, fund-raising letters, articles and books that come from the groups themselves.

Underlying Assumptions
Anyone who has followed the news reports about the New Christian Right since 1980 is aware of some of their particular issue stances. At a more fundamental level, however, it is important to see how these groups get to their specific positions. At the foundation of their platform are a number of crucial assumptions. It is to this foundation that we now turn our attention.

Politics as a Christian's business. First among these assumptions is the belief that all citizens and particularly Christian citizens have a responsibility to become involved in politics. This obligation stems not only from citizenship in a democratic political system but also, for Christians, from divine mandates. If this nation is in need of conversion, then politics can be used as one instrument of that conversion, and it is necessary for the right kinds of people to develop their political potential.

This call for political action is significant because for many years fundamentalist Christians had avoided political involvement; they had seen it as an evil endeavor that took time away from the more important goals of saving souls and building up the church. But the New Christian Right sought to mobilize Christians into a large and cohesive tool of national redemption. Consider these evocative words from one of the early statements by Christian Voice: "It is spiritually ignoble for the children of the King to lie down for a goring by the bulls of Satan. Such impotency violates the principles of the overcoming saints. God would have us be an army with banners flying. Have we become so mesmerized by the coming 'tribulation' that we have forgotten Christ's order to occupy *till I come?*"

This divine mandate, according to Christian Voice, does not call for just passive obedience to the powers of government, as some in the Christian community claim. The Bible calls for an active campaign to take control of the government and to use it to restore the nation's moral and spiritual health.

Ministers in particular have political responsibilities. According to the literature of the New Christian Right, every minister should do at least three things. First, the minister is to be a prophet, denouncing the sins of America just as Amos and Micah pointed out the sins of ancient Israel. On the basis of Ezekiel 3, Christian Voice warns: "God will hold accountable ministers who are unwilling to speak out in the midst of national evil." Second, the minister is to encourage the congregation to register to vote. Both the Moral

Majority and Christian Voice sent material to ministers outlining how they could arrange to have local government
officials come into their churches to register voters. In the
same breath Jerry Falwell has indicated that the function
of ministers is to preach the gospel of Jesus Christ and to
get people registered.

Finally, the minister's role is to educate the congregation
about current policy debates. Both organizations provide
ministers with detailed explanations of particular pieces
of legislation before Congress and urge them to share that
information with their churches. Of course, much of this
information has a definite point of view, but these groups
feel that they need to provide this perspective so that the
ministers can correctly interpret and react to the presenta-
tions made by the liberally controlled national news media.

In this respect, we will see in chapter six that many evangelical pastors are uncomfortable with such appeals from
the Moral Majority and Christian Voice. Their own role perceptions, formed during their years of training for the ministry, focus on religious rather than political persuasion.
Given this reluctance to be politically involved, one of the
greatest tasks of the New Christian Right has been and will
continue to be the development of new role perceptions.
Much of its success in turning this country around rests on
its effectiveness in reformulating ministerial functions.

Biblical morality as the cornerstone of a good society.   As a
Christian movement—despite the protestations of the Moral
Majority that they are not a religious organization—the New
Christian Right looks to the Bible for its political program.
These Christians believe that the Bible speaks directly to
contemporary issues. In laying out a series of divine prescriptions, the Bible provides twentieth-century believers
with a set of moral guidelines. By following these guidelines, Christians and the entire nation in which they live
will be blessed. In short, the underlying assumption is that

a strong society must manifest biblical morality; to the extent that people do not follow these prescriptions, their nation will weaken and probably collapse.

At this point the literature of the New Christian Right frequently quotes two verses of Scripture. The first is Proverbs 14:34: "Righteousness exalts a nation, but sin is a reproach to any people." The second is from 2 Chronicles 7:14: "If my people who are called by my name humble themselves, and pray and seek my face, and turn from their wicked ways, then I will hear from heaven, and will forgive their sin and heal their land." It was probably no coincidence that the Bible upon which President Reagan took the oath of office was open to this page in Chronicles. This set of verses explicitly links the following of biblical principles with national well-being. Not only will God's people be blessed, but their nation will also benefit. As Falwell puts it so succinctly, "It is right living that has made America the greatest nation on earth."[2]

When the people do not follow biblical morality, they suffer and so does the entire society. In the second chapter of his book *Listen, America!* Falwell documents the collapse of earlier empires when immorality reigned. The Christian Voice literature is full of statements linking the weakening position of the United States in the world community with the moral standards of the citizens. A fund-raising letter sent out in the fall of 1981 said:

Ever since atheist leader Madalyn Murray O'Hair had God kicked out of school, our children have suffered terribly. Today's schools produce millions of young criminals preying on the sick and elderly; dope addicts; illiterates; illegitimate mothers and hapless, vacant-eyed welfare dependents. And it's going to get worse, *much worse,* unless we Honor God by returning Him to our public schools. God is never going to bless a people that doesn't Honor Him before their children.

As another example of the same kind of historical interpretation, consider the claim frequently made that the United States has not won a war since the Supreme Court decisions against prayer and Bible reading in the public schools.

In short, because God only blesses those nations whose people live in accordance with biblical mandates, the solution to the social and economic problems of this country is obvious. The New Christian Right seeks to legislate its morality in the specific ways we will examine later.

A divine calling for the United States.   Several of the issue perspectives of Christian Voice and the Moral Majority demonstrate a strong commitment to the United States as a special nation. We have already observed Falwell's claim that the United States is the greatest nation on earth. Permeating the brochures and fund-raising letters of the groups is the notion that the United States is special not only because of its history of religious freedom but also for what it can do to fulfill God's purposes. The United States has a special mandate to be the instrument of God in the world.

Why is this country so crucial in God's plans? According to the New Christian Right, this country has three major tasks; if it fails, the kingdom of God will be set back terribly. The first task is to facilitate the evangelization of the whole world. Falwell puts it in stark terms: "North America is the last logical base for world evangelization."[3] It is not immediately clear whose logic is employed here, but it is clear that the United States must succeed. Falwell claims that this nation is in a unique position because it has the churches, the trained people, the money and the media facilities that are necessary to bring the gospel into all the world. The second task is to protect the nation of Israel. An early brochure put out by the Moral Majority asserted that "America is the only hope for the Jews in today's world." Later in the chapter we will examine why Israel is so important, but the point here is that without the United States the rest of the world would be endangered. The final task of this country is to protect the free world from the inevitable onslaught of the godless communists. Again we will look at the details of this responsibility later, but it is important to note here that this country is the only nation with enough military strength to deter or stop the attack.

Because the United States has these major responsibilities, it is vitally important to institute public policies which build and maintain American strength. That requires a clear and credible military strategy abroad, and a cohesive and prosperous society at home.

Liberty as the ultimate value. One of the things which makes the United States a great and strong country is its commitment to liberty—religious, political and economic. The importance of liberty in the life of Jerry Falwell is obvious: *Liberty* Baptist College situated upon *Liberty* Mountain. Reading through Falwell's glowing descriptions of our founding fathers almost sets the bells of freedom ringing in one's head. A 1981 brochure from the Moral Majority says it clearly: "We believe that liberty is the basic moral issue of all moral issues." Liberty is intimately tied with biblical morality because following biblical morality helps to protect our freedoms. To the extent that American citizens deviate from clear moral standards, they weaken themselves, they weaken their country and they consequently make the United States vulnerable to conquest. And conquest is bad because in it we sacrifice our freedom.

This commitment to liberty is perhaps best seen in the intense devotion to the free enterprise system of economics. The belief that individuals should be free to use their economic resources and talents as they see fit is central to many of the specific policy proposals of the New Christian Right. It is not just that a free market system is the best way to arrange economic relationships. Falwell contends that the Bible itself outlines the free enterprise system and the idea of property ownership.[4] Furthermore, he argues, attacks on business are really attacks on our whole economic system and thus ultimately attacks on freedom itself.

Limited role of government. Very closely related to the commitment to freedom is the perspective on the proper role of government in society. For the New Christian Right as for Thomas Jefferson, the best government is the government that does the least governing. One of the greatest dangers to personal freedom in contemporary America is the federal government. By usurping functions which had traditionally been done by the private sector, by accumulating powers to regulate business, schools and perhaps even churches, the federal government has long exceeded the bounds of propriety.

According to Falwell, the role of government is really quite clear: "When America was founded, the legitimate purpose of government was to protect the lives, the liberties, and the property of the citizens. It was not the purpose of government to redistribute resources or to enforce any particular results in the relationships and dealings of the citizenry among themselves."[5] This clearly represents a view of the government as a protector of rights rather than a promoter of rights. Such notions mirror the philosophy of the Republican Party and ideological conservatives.

How does the government act to protect people's rights? Two answers are given: first, by protecting citizens against foreign invasion, and, second, by protecting them from criminals at home. For Falwell the biblical passages presenting the duties of government mandate these two functions above all. And that is about all the government is charged with. There is no proper role for the government in equalizing income, in providing money or food to those who could be working, in educating children or in regulating business.[6] Given this philosophy, it is not surprising that Ronald Reagan was the preferred choice of the New Christian Right in the 1980 presidential election. What has gone wrong in the United States since the administration of Franklin Roosevelt is precisely that the government—and particularly the federal government—has attempted to do those things which people and business can and should do for themselves. Thus many of the groups' proposals call for dismantling certain government bureaucracies and re-establishing the government to its proper role as a servant of the people rather than their provider.

The battle between good and evil. Running through several of these assumptions is the idea that there is a clear distinction between the forces of good and evil. The warfare has begun, and unless dramatic things happen the forces of evil may triumph. Such a Manichean view of the world does not allow for any gray areas: people, events and ideas are either good or they are evil.

This warfare is reflected in two battles that are being waged today. The first battle pits the communists against those who believe in freedom. There is no redeeming social value in communism. The Russians as the leaders of the communist conspiracy are out to get us, and only a strong America can respond to the threat. The imagery of the conflict is most vivid in this comment from the Christian Voice Statement of Purpose: "We believe that America, the last stronghold of the Christian faith on this planet, has come under increasing attack from Satan's forces in recent years." For the New Christian Right the great battle described in the book of Revelation and predicted by some of the Old Testament writers is really the current cold-war struggle between the United States and the Soviet Union. Other nations have chosen or must choose sides. There is no middle ground in this ultimate conflict, no neutralism. Either a nation is on the side of the forces of good, or it is irredeemably evil.

The second battle is taking place within the United States itself; the combatants are moral Americans and liberal hu-

manists. The evil forces of humanism have taken control
of the powers of government—as well as the media and the
educational system—and are passing legislation that undermines the clear standards of biblical morality. The secular
humanists, as they are called, do not believe in God, they
do not believe in an unchangeable set of moral prescriptions and they do not believe in sin. Falwell states: "Humanism is man's attempt to create a heaven on earth, exempt-
ing God and His Law. Humanists propose that man is in
charge of his own destiny."[7] It is clear in the literature of the
New Christian Right that they see liberals as the epitome
of humanist thought and the authors of all that is wrong in
American society. Consider the following sentence in the
Christian Voice Statement of Purpose: "We believe that the
standards of Christian morality, the sanctity of our families,
the innocence of our young, and the very fiber of the Republic are crumbling under the onslaught of this powerful attack
launched by the 'rulers of darkness of this world,' and in-
sidiously sustained under the ever more liberal ethic."

In the mind of Jerry Falwell, these two battles—between
communism and freedom and between liberal humanism
and biblical morality—are inextricably linked. At several
points in his book he argues that policy proposals offered
by American liberals are really part of the worldwide communist conspiracy to sap our strength by undermining our
values. For example, he contends that the goals of those
promoting the Equal Rights Amendment are largely congruent with the objectives of socialism. For Falwell, there
is not much difference in being a communist, a socialist or
a liberal. They are all cut from the same cloth and represent a
very great danger. In short, these battles are not just struggles
between two basically acceptable sets of policies; these battles are much more fundamentally between good and evil.
The Bible is full of assurances about who will be the ultimate
victor in the battle, but the New Christian Right is not taking

any chances. It seeks to do battle right now, in the Decade of Destiny, to ensure the correct outcome. The remainder of this chapter will examine the specific choices they propose.

The Platform

One of the most unique features of this movement is the conviction that nearly all political issues have moral implications. Thus the New Christian Right makes proposals in areas that go beyond pornography, Sunday closings and alcoholic beverages. Their platform is wide ranging and substantially consistent with the preferences of ideological conservatives. We will examine their specific proposals in the following areas: foreign policy, economic policy, education and social issues.

Foreign policy. Many of the fundamental beliefs we just considered point to the need to maintain the military strength of the United States. If this country is to be successful in the inevitable conflict, our armed forces must be constantly ready and fully equipped. So the New Christian Right calls loudly for a significant increase in defense spending. Believing that the American defense capability has weakened because of our immoral living, the Moral Majority presents the grim consequences in one of their fund-raising letters: "And unless we re-build our military strength and keep a careful watch over the strength of our military position . . . one day the Russians may be able to pick up the telephone and call Washington, D.C., and dictate the terms of our surrender." Included in this letter was a petition to Congress calling for more defense money. While calling for military strength, the Moral Majority has rejected the 1982 Kennedy-Hatfield nuclear freeze proposal.

Some ambiguity remains in the New Christian Right position on defense spending in that they do not clearly indicate whether they favor a posture of military superiority or just military parity. They also do not indicate how much spending should rise, nor do they explicitly support particular weapons systems such as the MX missile or the B-1 bomber. In addition, Falwell mentions that he is dissatisfied with the current policy of containing the Soviets within their boundaries. Concluding a paragraph about the evils of Soviet communism, he writes: "But it appears that America's policy toward communism is one of containment, rather than victory."[8] It is not clear just how Falwell expects to achieve victory, but the implication is that we must move beyond a passive and reactive policy toward a more active effort to eliminate the threat. Such a policy would almost certainly require military superiority.

A second foreign policy issue that is dear to the hearts of group leaders is the unwavering support of Israel. A recent Moral Majority brochure lays it on the line: "One cannot belong to Moral Majority Inc. without making the commitment to support the state of Israel in its battle for survival and to support the human and civil rights of Jewish people everywhere." For many, including Falwell, this support is based on religious convictions: "Israel still stands as shining testimony to the faithfulness of God."[9] As God's chosen people Israel must survive, and the United States is uniquely equipped to assist. In fact, according to Falwell, one of the reasons why God has been so good to the United States is that this country has stood by Israel in the battles against her neighbors. Falwell expresses regret about the willingness of the United States in the 1970s to reduce its commitment to Israel in order to facilitate the flow of Arab oil. Although it is not clear whether the New Christian Right expects the United States to support everything Israel does—including establishing settlements in territories taken during the 1967 war—it is clear that our first commitment in the region must be the constant protection of the Jewish nation.

Finally, in keeping with a strong anticommunist stance of the New Christian Right, the United States should treat other nations in the world in such a way as to maximize our influence while minimizing that of the Soviets. This means two things.

In the first place it means that we must protect, support and equip those nations who are willing to join us in the battle against communism. Specifically, some people in the New Christian Right movement focus on Taiwan as one of America's most faithful partners in the cold-war struggle. They call upon this country to maintain our treaty relationship with Taiwan even if that undermines our incipient friendship with the mainland. Christian Voice has explicitly called for this policy; the Moral Majority, while denying that it has officially endorsed this proposal, has in fact included statements in its mailings that mourn the weakening ties with these anticommunists.

In the second place it means that the United States must refrain from making concessions to or supporting nations under the control of the international communist movement. Among the New Christian Right the focus is on two countries: Panama and Zimbabwe. Each of these countries is led by Marxists. Therefore the United States should not have signed the treaty giving Panama control of the canal, and the United States should continue the policy of economic sanctions against the Mugabe government. Again the Moral Majority denies that it has taken an official position on these issues, but their fund-raising letters speak explicitly about both.

The Manichean view of the world clearly provides the basis for the New Christian Right foreign policy prescriptions. Communism is the great evil; the United States is the great protector. There can be no middle ground: this country cannot flirt with the forces of evil, nor can it fail to support those who agree with us in this monumental battle. Israel, of course, is on our side, not only because it keeps a wary eye on the Soviets but also because it represents the forces of good in a more biblical sense.

Economics. Stemming from their commitment to a free enterprise system in which the government has only a small role, Christian Voice in particular has supported President Reagan in his program to cut government spending and to reduce income taxes. In fact, in June 1981 Christian Voice launched a National Christian Stewardship Campaign to encourage citizens to contact their legislators in support of these proposals. This campaign wanted, of course, the cuts to come from nondefense programs. The mass mailing called attention to the fact that federal money was going to a group of homosexuals in Los Angeles, a pornographer in Philadelphia and a project to produce a braille version of *Playboy*.

But underlying these specific targets was a devotion to government fiscal integrity: "Deficit spending—where government spends more than it takes in—is immoral; it violates every Biblical principle of good stewardship and living within one's means." Specifically, the group says that the tax cut program of the Reagan plan "will eventually mean thousands of your hard-earned dollars staying in your family budget where our provident Father intended them to be." Neither Falwell nor the Moral Majority is quite so outspoken about the Reagan program although both warn of the dangers of red ink in the federal budget.

Closely related to this is the notion that the government has been particularly misguided in its welfare policies which have been responsible for much of the deficit spending. One good way to restore fiscal integrity to the federal government would be to withdraw from these programs and turn welfare responsibilities over to families, churches and other charitable organizations. Falwell states: "Our whole welfare system is built on a basic premise that is detrimental to our society. We cannot survive economically when the working population of America is faced with an ever-increasing burden of governmental spending to support a tremendously large nonworking segment of our society."[10] Adhering rather strictly, but not without exception, to the biblical principle that those who do not work should not eat, Falwell laments the welfare dependency that has resulted from the liberal programs like food stamps.

Education. This same limited government philosophy also runs through a series of proposals concerning education. Freedom from governmental intrusion in private schools was, as we have seen, one of the crucial trigger events that led to the formation of both Christian Voice and the Moral Majority. It continues to be a rallying point as several private schools try to resist state attempts to mandate an acceptable curriculum, to require affirmative action in hiring teachers and to demand attendance records. At the heart of the groups' philosophy is the argument that education is the responsibility of the family rather than the government. Now that the majority of parents have forfeited their obligations, the opportunities for the state to shape the values and the lifestyles of little schoolchildren are greatly enhanced. Given the secular humanism which the New Christian Right sees as the religion taught in the public schools, these groups are vitally interested in protecting private schools and redeeming the public ones.

One of the battles in the field of education was lost during the Carter administration with the establishment of the cabinet Department of Education. The Christian Voice rating of legislators specifically favored those who voted against this department. They opposed its establishment, fearing that the department would be another step toward the control of local schools by the government and concerned that the department would reflect the humanism of the National Education Association.

In order to redeem public education, both groups have called for the re-establishment of voluntary prayer in public schools. Upset over the Supreme Court decision of two decades ago, Christian Voice goes even one step further by supporting a bill that would deny the Court jurisdiction over school policies. It will be interesting to see whether support for such a measure continues after Reagan has had the opportunity to appoint to the Court people reflecting his views about the proper role of the judiciary in American society.

In order to protect private schools, the groups have called on the government to exempt these institutions from affirmative action regulations in the hiring of teachers, especially to the extent that these promote the employment of known homosexuals. The groups feel that religious schools in particular must have the freedom to employ only those who uphold the moral standards which these schools teach. In addition, Christian Voice and the Moral Majority may be sympathetic to legislation that would provide tuition tax credits or tuition vouchers to parents who want to send their children to private schools. However, none of the groups has been very vocal about these tax or tuition measures, largely because many religious fundamentalists see these proposals as opening the door to more governmental involvement in private education.

Finally, the groups have opposed the use of busing to achieve the desegregation of schools. It is not immediately clear whether they oppose desegregation or whether they oppose busing as the means to achieve it, but Christian Voice has included the busing issue in its legislative report card. Their argument is that forced busing is expensive and that it undermines the concept of neighborhood schools and ultimately the concept of parental control over education. Senator Helms has been in the forefront of the antibusing movement in Congress; not so coincidentally the senator received a perfect score in the Christian Voice ratings.

Social issues.   Beyond all of this activity in the fields of defense policy, economics and education, it is really in the area of social policy that the New Christian Right has taken its stance and mobilized its constituency. Whether the motives be religious (as Christian Voice and Falwell claim) or moral (as the Moral Majority claims), the centerpiece of the movement is the effort to restore biblical morality to the United States.

Issue number one on the agenda is abortion. The sides were drawn in the 1973 Supreme Court decision that prohibited restrictions on a woman's right to have an abortion during the first three months of pregnancy. The Moral Majority calls the nearly 1.5 million abortions each year a "biological holocaust." The *Moral Majority Report* keeps its readers informed about new techniques for abortion and new congressional initiatives for halting this evil. The abortion struggle of late has focused on two points. One is the use of government funds to pay the cost of abortions for welfare mothers. Although the actual impact of the New Christian Right on this issue was minimal, the Supreme Court has declared that Congress may restrict these federal expenditures. The second point, which is more basic to the abortion issue, is the proposed Human Life Amendment to the Constitution. This amendment declares that life begins at the moment of conception, not at the moment of birth or at any other point during the pregnancy. The effect is to rule that abortion is murder. The proposal would do what the Supreme Court refused to do in 1973—determine the moment at which personhood, as protected by the Fifth and Fourteenth Amendments, begins. The road toward passage of a constitutional amendment is long and arduous, requiring not only special majorities in both houses of Congress but also ratification by 38 states. Despite these long odds, the New Christian Right is determined to make its claims about abortion heard and legislated.

The second agenda item is homosexuality. We have already observed that the groups have resisted any mandate to private schools to hire homosexual teachers. Christian

Voice and Jerry Falwell argue that homosexuality is unnatural; according to Falwell, "the sin of homosexuality is so grievous, so abominable in the sight of God, that He destroyed the cities of Sodom and Gomorrah because of this terrible sin."[11] While claiming not to oppose homosexuals as persons or to oppose civil rights for homosexuals, the New Christian Right does oppose treating homosexuals as an official minority group like Blacks or Hispanics. Were the groups to have their way on this issue, homosexuality would not be a criterion for affirmative action plans, and it would be very difficult to prove legally any discrimination against them in terms of housing or employment. Furthermore, the New Christian Right is vehemently against certifying marriages between homosexuals and allowing homosexual partners to adopt children.

A third issue is feminism. Here the position of the Moral Majority is virtually a carbon copy of the 1980 Republican Party platform. Each group expresses support for equal rights defined in terms of pay, advancement and educational opportunities, but contends that the Equal Rights Amendment is not the proper way to achieve this. The argument is that the proposed amendment is too vague. Falwell, for example, goes into great detail in his book to "prove" that passing the ERA will mean that women will be drafted, that all restrooms will be sexually integrated and that homosexual marriages will be legal. Despite legal arguments to the contrary, the groups are so convinced of these consequences that they have joined forces in many states with anti-ERA movements. In addition, Falwell argues that many leaders of the ERA movement are actually socialists, which is enough evidence for him that their value systems are faulty.

The Moral Majority and Christian Voice also speak strongly against pornography, and Falwell has been a participant in an unsuccessful lawsuit against *Penthouse* magazine over an interview with him that was published in that forum.

Although the specific position on pornography is ambiguous, some parts of the movement call for stricter enforcement of existing pornography laws, especially those restrictions on selling it to children. The Moral Majority has also participated in a coalition which threatened television advertisers who market products on certain offensive shows. Aside from a general wish to do away with pornography and some local efforts to defeat looser restrictions, the New Christian Right has not yet specified any criteria by which to measure pornography. Nor has it called for national legislation that would completely ban everything that it labels as offensive.

The final social issue which concerns the groups is crime. While this is really a different kind of social issue, they do see interrelationships between crime, pornography, unstable family patterns and drug trafficking. Christian Voice proclaims its support for capital punishment, saying that it is a biblical approach to crime. Falwell says that the threat of death is a deterrent to crime. None of the groups, however, makes this a big issue.

In addition, Falwell has expressed his opposition to gun control and the Moral Majority has passed up several opportunities to call for handgun restrictions in their coverage of the attempted assassination of President Reagan in March 1981. The *Moral Majority Report* has also kept its readers informed about attempts in Congress to revise the criminal code. The group was particularly incensed about proposals to reduce the penalties for so-called victimless crimes—gambling, prostitution and other kinds of sexual behavior between consenting adults—and with proposals that would make pornography prosecutions more difficult.

Summary
The platform of the New Christian Right is certainly more comprehensive in its coverage than that of other religious groups. One of the strengths of this movement has been its

ability to ally with other groups which have been working on specific issues for a longer time. At the outset of the chapter we noted that there are some differences within the New Christian Right about specific policy stances. The table below indicates which people and groups have expressed opinions about a series of issues. The information in table 1 comes from contacts with group leaders, media interviews with the leaders, books or articles written by people within the groups, and brochures and mass mailings from the groups. Given the impossibility of reading or hearing everything that the leaders have said, the table may err in a conservative direction. That is to say, while every preference listed has actually been expressed at some time since 1979, other preferences not available for this research may also have been stated.

As we can see, the differences within the movement are quite small. There is a substantial degree of unity about issue positions which certainly represents a source of strength for these groups. The table also indicates the relevant positions from the 1980 Republican Party platform. It is clear that the New Christian Right and the conservatives within the Republican Party have much in common.

Issue	Christian Voice	Moral Majority	Jerry Falwell	Republican Party
Foreign Policy				
Anticommunism	X	X	X	X
More defense spending	X	X	X	X
Protect Israel		X	X	X
Oppose Panama Canal Treaty			X	
Maintain friendship with Taiwan	X	X		X
Sanctions on Zimbabwe	X			
No negotiations with Palestine Liberation Organization		X		X
Economic Policy				
Support free enterprise	X	X	X	X
Welfare as a private concern		X	X	
Support balanced budget	X	X	X	X
Support Reagan tax and spending cuts	X			X
Education				
Family responsibility	X	X	X	X
Oppose busing	X			X
Voluntary prayer in public schools	X	X	X	X
Oppose Department of Education	X			X
Maintain tax exemptions for private schools	X	X	X	X
Oppose hiring homosexual teachers		X	X	
Social Issues				
Support Human Life Amendment	X	X	X	X
Oppose abortion on demand	X	X	X	X
No federal money for welfare abortions	X			X
Oppose ERA		X	X	X
Support death penalty	X		X	X
Oppose gun control			X	X
Stricter enforcement of pornography laws		X	X	
Oppose homosexuality as class of minorities	X	X	X	

Table 1. Groups Advocating Issue Stances

4
The Politics of Interest Groups

CHRISTIAN VOICE AND THE MORAL Majority are contemporary examples of a phenomenon which has long fascinated journalists and scholars: pressure-group politics. These two organizations are composed of people who share a set of interests and who seek to make government policy responsive to those interests. In this sense the groups are similar to hundreds of other groups trying to persuade public officials that their vision for this nation is the best one. Thus we can learn more about these two groups by looking at what others have observed about interest groups in general. In this chapter we will examine the nature of interest-group politics in the United States, discuss the organizational dynamics associated with the establishment and continuance of these two groups, and review the strategies and tactics employed, particularly grassroots lobbying and the legislative report card.

Interest-Group Politics in the United States

The overall attitude about interest groups in this country is highly paradoxical. Some people see interest groups as a very important and prominent part of our political system. According to these observers, interest groups function as interest aggregators and interest articulators. By pulling together a number of people who, perhaps unknowingly, share common concerns and similar preferences, interest groups provide a forum for those who could not be as effective through their own individual political actions. Furthermore, by facilitating the expression of those shared interests, these groups play a crucial role in allowing the government to hear and respond to the opinions of its citizens. That interest groups are useful instruments of democracy can be seen in the fact that almost two-thirds of American adults belong to at least one group. Several studies of legislative decision making have shown that elected officials look to interest groups as an indication of how citizens respond to proposed bills.

On the other hand, however, Americans also are suspicious of groups. The term "pressure-group politics" is sure to evoke negative images of lobbyists lurking in the halls of Congress waiting to pounce on some vulnerable legislator with illicit rewards for specific votes. In this perspective interest groups are seen as selfishly concerned only with their own narrow interests and all-powerful in the arena of government. The political decisions that result ignore what is in the interest of the country as a whole while maximizing the advantages that accrue to the victorious pressure group. Throughout our history the media have been filled with stories about how our elected officials dance to the tune of rich and sinister lobbyists who care little about the public interest.

Interest groups can be seen either as crucial tools of democracy through which citizens make known their opinions or as selfish manipulators. The tension between these two views has persisted ever since the founding fathers attempted to construct a government. Perhaps some of the ambivalence of Americans toward the New Christian Right in the 1980s has its roots in this very paradox. New Christian Right supporters praise the groups for giving them the opportunity to persuade policy makers; the opponents wonder whether the groups should be allowed to push their own brand of morality on everyone. Is the New Christian Right a medium of popular expression, protected by the constitutional rights to assemble and petition the government? Or is the New Christian Right a loud, self-serving band of zealots who unfairly coerce legislators with threats of election hit lists and divine judgment? In light of the differing views about interest groups in general, we may never be able to answer these questions to everyone's satisfaction.

The New Christian Right, then, finds its place in a long line of groups which have attempted to influence public policy in the United States. Is there anything unique about this particular movement? Is it just like all the others, or is this movement something new and fresh? Those who have studied interest groups find that most groups are organized to achieve a rather tangible goal.[1] For example, a labor union is formed to obtain certain economic benefits such as higher wages or better fringe benefits. Likewise, farmers have established organizations which push for higher price supports or more favorable inheritance tax laws. Manufacturers join forces in calling for protective tariffs, depreciation allowances or fewer regulations. All of these groups seek to achieve policies resulting in greater material benefits for themselves.

Groups like the Moral Majority and Christian Voice clearly do not fall in the same category. They do not call for policies which will distribute benefits mostly to their own members, nor do they concentrate on bills in just one policy area. In contrast, they focus on legislation that sets up or maintains a moral structure for political, economic or social interrelationships.[2] They call not just for financial or physical health but for moral and spiritual health. Their concern is not just for their own members but the entire society. Because Christian Voice and the Moral Majority do not fit the traditional interest-group mold, we must look for other theories to explain their existence.

Social scientists have already offered some alternative explanations. One of the more extreme assessments comes from Richard Hofstadter, who argues that radical groups form as anti-intellectual and irrational responses to change.[3] A more moderate and useful theory to explain the New Christian Right sees their emergence as a rational response to an attack on their lifestyles and value systems. According to this theory, the Moral Majority and Christian Voice were formed to defend their beliefs and to achieve government policies which would legitimate their values.[4] Fairbanks argues that the temperance movement and the modern fundamentalist movement were "both attempting to maintain an older concept of morality based on traditional religion against the claims of a new morality brought on by the forces of modernization. . . . Both movements sought symbolic recognition of the validity of their values through victories in battles over constitutional amendments."[5]

Like an economic interest group which turns to political involvement in order to achieve its tangible goal, so too the New Christian Right is turning to politics to achieve its intangible, but not irrational, goal of preserving and legitimating its value system. What motivates people to join and contribute to these groups is not some promise of material gain but the identification with a cause that for many seems more important than money or objects. These people are willing to sacrifice in order to continue the struggle against the devil, whether manifested in international communism or domestic liberalism. The groups' intensity stems from the depths of their commitment; it is likely to fade only with legislative successes or with the appearance of a dramatic economic or foreign policy crisis that demands immediate and total attention.

Tactics

The groups associated with the New Christian Right have employed the whole range of instruments which interest groups traditionally use to achieve their objectives. However, their strong tie to the electronic church, their nature as a mass-based movement and their relative lack of experience in partisan politics dictate that they emphasize some tactics rather than others. Although each group has a Washington office which makes direct contacts with members of Congress, the major focus of their efforts has been what political scientists call grassroots lobbying. This kind of lobbying involves activating their group members to petition individual legislators rather than relying on direct contact between a paid lobbyist and a legislator. Grassroots lobbying rests on the assumption that elected officials are more concerned with the views of their constituents than with the opinions of a registered lobbyist. Therefore, constituents have greater access, by letter or by visit, to a legislator than does a lobbyist with few ties to the electoral district.

When a bill comes up in Congress, an interest group seeks to mobilize its membership to contact their representatives. Usually this takes the form of a stimulated letter-writing campaign; in many instances the group will provide sample letters or postcards which the members can sign and mail to Washington. It is clear that recent developments in mass-mailing techniques makes these letter campaigns much easier. Both Christian Voice and the Moral Majority have launched these kinds of efforts, urging citizens to write to members of Congress and even to the president on behalf of or usually in opposition to specific bills. On the surface at least, the Moral Majority has tremendous potential in this respect because its membership is so geographically dispersed that it automatically has access to most members of Congress.

Most legislators would admit that massive outpourings of mail on a particular topic—especially if most of it is urging the same action—may affect their decisions. Such outpourings are one measure of the intensity of constituent opinions when other indicators such as public opinion polls are not available. In addition, participation in these campaigns helps to give citizens a feeling of involvement in their government, often at very little personal cost. Even if the decision should go against their preference, they can say they tried. Research done by social scientists suggests, however, that many legislators do not take seriously a flood of letters that appears to have been stimulated by an interest group.[6] Since on most issues legislators receive very few letters, it is easy to detect stimulated mail: several letters with similar —or identical—content descend all at once. So when the deluge hits, many legislators are likely to discount the opinion expressed as stimulated rather than genuine.

How can we reconcile this inconsistency between the increasing use of such mail campaigns and the research conclusions that they may not be very effective? One way would be to argue that groups sponsor such letter-writing campaigns primarily for the symbolism they convey: the symbolism of intensity when thousands of letters hit Capitol Hill, the symbolism of participation when citizens take this direct action or the symbolism of representation when legislators can use these letters as justifications for doing what they would have done anyway. There is some validity to this notion.

Another idea is also plausible. It could be that at some point in terms of numbers of letters, a legislator would finally say that the opinions expressed seem so prevalent that it would be the better part of political wisdom to respond positively. The argument here would suggest that small mail campaigns appear to be so easy to execute that opinion could in fact be stimulated, but that large campaigns require such extensive and intensive efforts that the constituents must be fully aware of what they are doing and that they may well remember this particular congressional vote at the next election. At that point, a legislator may perceive the issue to be political survival, regardless of the ratio of spontaneity to outside stimulation.

In addition to these indirect contacts with members of Congress, both Christian Voice and the Moral Majority have small staffs of registered lobbyists who meet individually with legislators or staff members and who provide testimony at committee hearings. The Christian Voice lobbying staff, led by Gary Jarmin, has petitioned legislators about a variety of issues, with a concentration of efforts on school prayer, homosexuality and Reagan's economic program. In like manner Moral Majority lobbyists have been active in campaigns against proposed revisions of the criminal code and in favor of the Family Protection Act and the Human Life Amendment.

Most people, however, do not recognize the Moral Majority because of these direct or indirect contacts with legislators. Rather the group's fame was secured in the 1980 elections as it sought to register new voters and to educate them about the issues in the campaign. Although the story of these electoral exploits is well known, it bears repeating.

Both Christian Voice and the Moral Majority participated in voter registration drives during the election year. Polls had shown that fundamentalists had a much lower turnout rate than some of the other groups and that many were not even registered. So the groups decided that registration would be a top priority. To accomplish this, they relied extensively on local pastors to convince their congregations that they had obligations to register and vote. The assumption, probably correct, was that churchgoers would respond more positively to their own pastors than to a national organization. The groups held seminars and sent special mailings to ministers providing them with appropriate information about the registration process. In many instances the pastors were able to arrange for county registration officials to come directly into the church to add people's names to the voting rolls. Falwell claims to have registered over 3 million new voters in 1980, although the claim could probably not be validated.

While registration was one priority, a second was the education of the voters. Both groups conducted large campaigns to convince voters that some candidates were better than others. Again the groups depended on pastors to present the political message to their churches. Obviously neither group had the resources to mount an effective campaign in every state; so they selected those races in which a prominent liberal was vulnerable, as they saw it, to a conservative challenger. Christian Voice specifically targeted about 35 key races; the Moral Majority focused on fewer than a dozen. Tons of literature portraying the liberal candidates as immoral officials flowed into these election districts.

We saw how federal election laws put limits on how much an organization could contribute to any candidate, but the law has two big loopholes. One is that groups may spend as much as they want on negative campaigns, appeals against one of the candidates rather than for another. So in Iowa, the groups targeted John Culver; in South Dakota, George McGovern was their victim; in Indiana, it was Birch Bayh; in California, Alan Cranston was on the hit list. The second loophole allows groups to spend unlimited amounts on behalf of candidates as long as their efforts are not coordinated with those of the candidate's official campaign committee.

One of the most visible ways to educate voters was to send people a report card on their own representative's voting record in Congress. Christian Voice, as perhaps the most prominent example, selected fourteen moral issues on which Congress had voted in 1979, including abortion, school busing, prayer in public schools and U.S. relations with Taiwan. Having identified the correct moral vote on each issue, they could then calculate a morality rating for every legislator, ranging from zero to one hundred. For example, in the Senate the highest scores were given to Armstrong (Colorado), Laxalt (Nevada), Humphrey (New Hampshire) and Helms (North Carolina). Several senators received ratings of zero, indicating that they had voted incorrectly on every one of the fourteen issues. Included in this group were Cranston (California), Hart (Colorado), Bayh (Indiana), Culver (Iowa), Kennedy and Tsongas (Massachusetts) and McGovern (South Dakota). This information was sent to voters in the target states along with appeals to get these "immoral" people out of office. Another report card was issued in 1982, targeting for defeat such people as Weicker (Connecticut), Moynihan (New York), Kennedy (Massachusetts) and Riegle (Michigan). Although the Moral Majority did not have its own morality ratings and claimed not to have a hit list, they did provide information about legislators' votes to citizens in selected states.

In addition to these educational efforts, New Christian Right groups reached churchgoers with their leafletting campaigns in church parking lots on the Sunday before the election. After these congregants had just heard a sermon about their political responsibilities, it was significant that they would be immediately confronted with the literature of the New Christian Right. Much of this activity was performed not by the national organizations but by state offshoots. A leading member of Iowans for Moral Government, a Moral Majority group, confessed to the Des Moines Register that some of their leaflets had come straight from the Republican National Committee.[7]

When there is not an election right around the corner, both Christian Voice and the Moral Majority work to build up their memberships and rally their troops. For example, the Moral Majority produces a monthly newspaper called the *Moral Majority Report*, with a circulation of over 1 million, although some recipients report getting multiple copies. This newspaper is a blend of objective reporting about the status of legislation and more sensationalistic stories outlining the latest conspiracies against which they must fight. The group sponsors in addition occasional radio and newspaper reports focusing on more specific topics, such as a bill that is being debated in Congress. Christian Voice too has sponsored short radio spots presenting their ideas and soliciting new members. They also regularly send their *Legislative Alert* to ministers so that these religious leaders can keep their congregations informed about current issues.

The Moral Majority and its affiliated state organizations have conducted seminars to train local leaders and potential candidates for office. For instance, the Legal Defense Foundation held a three-day conference in September 1981 on pornography. Inviting lawyers, community leaders and politicians, they discussed ways to encourage better enforcement of existing laws. They talked about boycotting firms that advertise, distribute or sell such materials. Five months later the organization sponsored two conferences designed to provide election skills for potential candidates and other interested political activists. As a smaller organization, Christian Voice has not been as active as the Moral Majority in this area, but they have helped to establish the national project Prayer Coalition, an alliance of about 50 organizations seeking to reinstitute voluntary prayer in the public schools.

Finally, both groups have been involved in the nationwide

campaign to clean up American TV programs. Working with the Rev. Don Wildmon, leader of the Coalition for Better Television and member of the Christian Voice national advisory committee, they have threatened to boycott the sponsors of programs that show offensive material, generally measured by the extent to which the behavior of the characters goes against the standards of biblical morality.

Following a period of television viewing in early 1980 and several announcements of impending boycotts, the coalition was successful in getting one of the largest advertisers, Proctor and Gamble, to withdraw its sponsorship of certain programs. In addition, in December 1981 Christian Voice sent a mailing to its members asking them to boycott ABC programs for one week in protest against a show about television preachers. However, when in 1982 Wildmon's coalition called for a boycott of NBC and products from affiliated companies (RCA and Hertz), the Moral Majority refused to go along. Starting its own campaign, the group developed Clean Up Television Kits for members; the kits included addresses of major advertisers as well as sample letters which viewers could send to sponsors and networks. Here again the New Christian Right jumped aboard a movement that had been going on for several years.

Some of the harshest criticism of the groups has come from those who see the threat of boycotts as a form of censorship and a denial of free speech. But such activities are entirely consistent with the New Christian Right thesis that moral standards have declined and that the absence of such standards is a distinct threat to our national survival.

Conclusions

It is very difficult to measure the effectiveness of interest groups, either in their efforts to elect certain people to office or in their attempts to get certain bills through the Congress. The great difficulty for social scientists is to determine whether voters or legislators would have behaved the same way even if the interest groups had not acted. In view of this difficulty, some analysts have fallen back on the theory that where there is much activity there must be some influence. If that theory has any validity at all, the New Christian Right must have had a large impact on recent American politics. They have certainly been among the most active groups.

Yet action is not the same as influence. If influence is defined as getting someone to change his or her mind, rather than reinforcing a conviction already held, then we have reason to argue that the New Christian Right may not be as influential as some of its leaders suggest or some of its detractors fear. One could argue that the Moral Majority and Christian Voice are simply riding along on the tide of conservatism that has marked the country since the late 1970s. Perhaps their perceived success is the result of, rather than the cause of, Reagan's nomination, election and legislative victories. We must take a much closer look at the 1980 elections to see whether the New Christian Right has had any independent effect on American politics.

5
The First Test:
The 1980 Elections

"I THINK THAT THESE CHRISTIAN people came out of the pews into the polls and caused this avalanche."[1] With these words Jerry Falwell tried to explain one of the most stunning election outcomes since World War 2. We have already noted that the 1980 presidential and congressional elections were the first test of strength for the New Christian Right, and the results bear witness to a significant potential. Ronald Reagan had been the choice of 51 per cent of those who voted, and he had won just under 91 per cent of the Electoral College votes. President Carter had won pluralities in only five states and in the District of Columbia.

What had seemed to be such a close election turned into a landslide. Caught in this avalanche were a number of liberal senators and representatives whose defeat was crucial to the Republican capture of the U.S. Senate and the whittled ·

Democratic majority in the House. The election outcome sent
the analysts scurrying to find the causes of this surprising
victory. They especially wanted to know how much effect
groups like Christian Voice and the Moral Majority had had.
In this chapter we will assess the impact of the New Christian Right in the 1980 elections, looking first at the national
results and then focusing on an important litmus-test election in Iowa matching incumbent John Culver and challenger Charles Grassley.

It is quite difficult to provide definitive answers about the
impact of any one group or issue in an election. Studies of
voting behavior attest to the complexity of the choosing process, especially in situations where multiple pressures are
competing for the voter's attention. Probably the best data
available to answer questions about the impact of these
groups on the election are polls of citizens taken as they
left the voting booths on November 4, 1980. Several organizations conducted such polls, and so we do have some important evidence about voter perceptions.

Even these data, however, are not completely adequate
because the categories used to distinguish among respondents are not as precise as we would like. That is, the polling
organizations are not able to tell us how much members of
New Christian Right groups supported Reagan in 1980; the
best they can do is to indicate Reagan's support among Protestants in general, white Protestants or evangelicals. None
of these categories perfectly matches the list of New Christian Right supporters. Furthermore, election analysis requires that we look back to previous elections so that we may
see whether any particular pattern of voting in one election
is similar to or different from the patterns found in earlier
elections. Unfortunately, in 1976 polling organizations were
even more general in their categories: most did not distinguish between evangelical Protestants and other Protestants,
so that we have little basis for comparing the data from 1976

and 1980. In short, it will be nearly impossible to "prove" or "disprove" the thesis that the New Christian Right had a significant impact in the election of Ronald Reagan and a Republican Senate.

National Patterns
In the light of these problems it is easy to understand why conclusions about the impact of these groups range all over the scale, from the statement by Falwell attributing the conservative landslide to churchgoers, to several more pessimistic arguments that the New Christian Right floated along on a conservative tide that they had no part in creating. Vague and unsatisfactory though it be, perhaps the assessment by Houston pollster Lance Tarrance is the best we can achieve: "The effect of the Moral Majority is not as great as is claimed, but more than its detractors care to admit."[2]

Looking first at the presidential contest, it was clear that all three major candidates could lay claim to the votes of evangelicals. Reagan, of course, had the blessing of the New Christian Right leadership and the endorsement of the Christian Voice Moral Government Fund, but Carter had developed a solid evangelical base in the 1976 campaign, and Anderson was quite well known in Christian circles.

Nearly all the surveys taken on election day included a question about the religious preferences of the respondents. The conclusions are quite similar. It is clear that Reagan won a majority of the Protestant vote and, more specifically, he won a majority of the born-again vote (among both Protestants and Catholics). For example, the New York Times/CBS News poll showed that Reagan won 61 per cent of the votes of born-again white Protestants; Carter won another 35 per cent, and Anderson claimed only 3 per cent. Among all-white Protestants Reagan won 60 per cent with Carter securing another 30 per cent and Anderson getting 8 per cent.[3] Unfortunately, the comparable 1976 election day poll did not differentiate among Protestants, so we cannot reach any conclusions about whether these data from 1980 indicate a trend. The more inclusive data we have from 1976 and 1980 show that Carter's share of the total Protestant vote declined 7 per cent in the four years, from a high of 63 per cent in 1976 to 56 per cent in 1980.

At this point interpretations differ. What is clear is that Reagan did better than President Ford among Protestants, but it is also clear that Reagan did better than Ford among almost every group in society. In this respect it is important to notice that born-again Protestants did not vote differently from all white Protestants in 1980. Everett Carll Ladd's analysis of these data leads him to argue: "Jimmy Carter actually received a slightly higher proportion of the born-again Protestant vote than of the vote of other Protestants."[4] On these grounds he concludes, "Born-again Christians simply are not more conservative than other Christians, and they did not vote differently in 1980."[5] Similar explanations of the impact of the New Christian Right were offered by Lipset and Raab[6] and by Castelli.[7] Interestingly, the pollsters for both the Reagan and the Carter campaign organizations attributed only marginal significance to the efforts of the Moral Majority.[8]

On the other hand, however, there is some evidence that Baptists thoroughly repudiated Carter in 1980; and because Baptists form a crucial part of the New Christian Right constituency, there may have been some impact. For example, the ABC News/Louis Harris survey on election day demonstrated that Reagan won the Baptist vote by 56 to 34 per cent, but that four years earlier Carter had won 56 per cent of these votes. Certainly this marked a turnabout which would lead us to question the conclusions discussed above. Harris claimed that two-thirds of Reagan's popular vote margin came from the followers of the television preachers.[9] Yet it is not accurate to measure New Christian Right support by

looking only at Baptist votes, since Baptists tend to be highly
ambivalent about the Moral Majority and Christian Voice.

These data, inconsistent as they are, still do not provide
us with an accurate measure of the groups' influence because
they do not tell us that vote shifts resulted from the appeals
of the groups rather than from other factors. In other words,
we need to know whether these voters would have pulled
the Republican lever even if the New Christian Right had
not sought their support. This question too is impossible to
answer with any precision, but we do have some evidence
about the reasons some people gave for voting the way they
did. Nearly every postelection analysis attributed the Reagan
victory to dissatisfaction with Carter's performance in office
rather than to confidence that Reagan could do much better.
A postelection poll taken by the Roper organization, for example, found that only 43 per cent of Reagan voters expressed a "good deal of enthusiasm" about the candidate.[10]
The *New York Times*/CBS News poll showed that only half
of the voters picked a candidate because they liked him.[11]
The election then was not so much an expression of support
for Reagan as an expression of discontent with Carter.

Furthermore, to the extent that issues played a role in the
election, it was clear that the social agenda of the New Christian Right was not foremost in the minds of voters. Most analysts contend that the key issues were economic, with inflation topping the list of concerns, followed by unemployment. Although the New Christian Right, and particularly
Christian Voice, had included economic issues in their appeals, their major focus was not on these issues.

In summary, an examination of these data lead to the conclusion that the Moral Majority and Christian Voice probably
did have some role in the Reagan victory, but that their efforts
were only a small part of the overall movement in a conservative direction. Certainly Reagan did well among fundamentalists and evangelicals, but he did well among almost every

social group. Certainly there was a turnabout among evangelicals between 1976 and 1980, but there was a comparable switch among most groups. The conclusion by Lipset and Raab seems most accurate:

What all these findings seem to indicate is that the efforts to mobilize a religious constituency for political purposes in America had no measurable effect on the 1980 elections. Instead, the available evidence appears to sustain the thesis that the electoral swing toward conservatism and the emergence of a political evangelical movement were parallel developments which may have been mutually reinforcing rather than related to one another as cause and effect.[12]

If the New Christian Right aided but did not cause the Reagan victory, what about the congressional campaigns in which several liberal Democrats lost their seats to conservative Republicans? Its impact in these races is even harder to assess because we lack comparable survey data from many of the states. In the absence of these data we can see who won but not necessarily why they won.

There is no doubt, however, that the New Christian Right was very active in congressional elections in several states. Christian Voice, working through its political action committee, targeted just over 30 races, most of them featuring a liberal Democratic incumbent facing a conservative Republican challenger. It is more difficult to discern where the Moral Majority focused its efforts because the organization did not endorse candidates. Reports from several states, however, indicate that the group was active in almost a dozen states, concentrating on key Senate races. Although the national organization did not endorse candidates, state affiliates did make their preferences known and much of the "educational" material produced and distributed by the group left few doubts about which candidate was better.

From the results of these campaigns the New Christian

Right was apparently quite successful. *U.S. News and World Report* indicated that 23 of 38 legislators with low ratings on the Christian Voice report cards were defeated.[13] In addition, most of the targeted liberal senators lost, including Bayh, Church, Culver, McGovern and Nelson. Only a few survived, among them Cranston, Hart and Eagleton. These results were particularly amazing when we consider the overwhelming success which incumbents usually enjoy: in House races about 90 per cent of those incumbents who seek re-election are successful, while among senators the record is about two-thirds.[14] If the normal course of affairs is for incumbents to win, then how can we explain the 1980 election returns?

One explanation revolves around the New Christian Right. Candidates in both Alabama (Jeremiah Denton) and Oklahoma (Don Nickles) attributed the results in part at least to the efforts of the Moral Majority in those two states. Folsom, the defeated candidate in Alabama, said that the group had a "tremendous effect on my defeat."[15] Senator Denton's rise from relative obscurity to victory was certainly aided by the publicity of the Moral Majority.

On the other hand, there are some reasons to discount the claims of New Christian Right effectiveness in these races. For one thing, other candidates indicated less impact for these groups when talking about their victories or defeats. Senator McGovern, although bitter enough about his defeat to form a new group to counteract the National Conservative Political Action Committee and the Moral Majority, said that the religious groups were not responsible for his defeat. McGovern's opponent, Representative James Abdnor, in fact expressed irritation about some New Christian Right activities which, he felt, did more to hurt his campaign than to help it by diverting attention away from the issues he was stressing.

Statements made by candidates are generally not the best

evidence on which to base an assessment of the effects of groups in the campaign. In the desire of a newly elected official to establish a base of support, he or she is likely to include within the base as many groups as possible. In contrast, defeated candidates may attempt to rationalize their losses by providing alternative explanations, particularly in cases like these where morality was such an issue. Thus we must look for other evidence.

One possibility again is that certain candidates would have won even without the activities of the New Christian Right in their district. The congressional elections could be seen as a series of repudiations of incumbent legislators much as Reagan's vote can be seen as an anti-Carter vote. Or the elections could be seen as a Republican victory rather than a New Christian Right victory. Evidence for this notion comes from the Lipset and Raab study which compared the votes in these targeted states with the votes elsewhere. They concluded: "But the decline in their vote was *almost identical* with that of the Democratic senatorial candidates in eighteen non-targeted states in the north. The average vote for the five liberal Senators fell from 54.5 per cent in 1974 to 48 in 1980; the Democratic senatorial vote in the eighteen other northern contests declined from 55 percent to 48" (emphasis theirs).[16]

In summary, there are substantial difficulties in assessing the impact of these groups in the 1980 elections, and our conclusions must therefore be quite tentative. It would be helpful if polling organizations had written their questions in such a way as to tap the views of New Christian Right supporters, but that must wait for future elections. As for the 1980 election, groups such as the Christian Voice and the Moral Majority were certainly pleased by the outcome, and they did have a small role to play in bringing about the results. Given the margins of victory in the presidential contest and in many senatorial races, however, we cannot conclude that the New Christian Right was a decisive factor. There were too many other factors pointing in the same direction. In a few close races their efforts may have made the difference, but the available data do not allow us to confirm that.

The Iowa Senate Election

Perhaps an effective way to look at the impact of the New Christian Right would be to look more closely at one election in which the groups were active. Voters in Iowa were confronted with a clear choice in the 1980 senatorial election. On the one hand was incumbent Democrat John Culver. Schooled at Harvard, he worked for a while on the staff of Senator Edward Kennedy before seeking a House seat in 1964. Ten years later he won a Senate seat when Harold Hughes resigned. Culver's voting records in both the House and the Senate were quite liberal considering the strong Republican Party in his home state. When Christian Voice presented its report card, Culver was at the bottom: he had not voted correctly on a single issue. Political analysts in Iowa increasingly believed that 1980 would be a tough fight, particularly since two years earlier another liberal incumbent, Senator Dick Clark, had been ousted by conservative Roger Jepsen.

Culver's opponent, Charles Grassley, presented a sharp contrast. A local boy, Grassley had attended universities in Iowa and had farmed while serving in the state legislature and the U.S. House of Representatives. His voting record was consistently conservative, and Christian Voice gave him a 100 per cent rating. As a Baptist, Grassley spent many Sundays during the campaign talking in churches throughout the state. When the voting took place in November, Grassley had outpolled Culver 54 to 46 per cent.

A survey of evangelical pastors (see chapter six) found that both Christian Voice and the Moral Majority were active in the contest, as well as the National Conservative Political

Action Committee and right-to-life groups. NCPAC spent $149,000 in a campaign to defeat Culver. Several Christian Voice supporters set up an organization called Christians for Grassley, and the statewide chapter of the Moral Majority distributed literature comparing the issue stances of the two candidates. Although this group did not officially endorse Grassley, ministers in Iowa indicated that their educational materials were clearly slanted in the challenger's direction. As a result of this activity, Erling Jorstad commented: "The strongest show of New Christian Right muscle turned up in Iowa."[17]

Activity is not the same thing as influence, as we have said. A comprehensive examination of the movement's impact would require information about county vote totals and information about where the local efforts were most intense. The latter data are not available, but we can learn some important things by looking at the county election data for 1974 (Culver's first Senate race) and for 1980. Culver's overall decline was 7.85 per cent statewide, showing a decline in 90 of Iowa's 99 counties.

One hypothesis would predict that Culver lost the most votes in those counties with high percentages of potential New Christian Right supporters and that he did best in those areas not likely to support these groups. Assuming the Baptists would tend to be more supportive, we can look at whether counties with relatively large numbers of Baptist churches voted against Culver. Iowa does not have a large number of Baptists, but in those counties with more than three Baptist churches, Culver's percentage decrease was 7.5, or slightly lower than his statewide decrease. Looking specifically at the data from those counties represented on the Iowans for Moral Government Executive Committee, Culver's percentage decrease was 6.4, again lower than the statewide average. It is difficult to interpret these figures as an indication of New Christian Right muscle.

If the counties with relatively more Baptists were not the source of Culver's defeat, where did he lose his support from the earlier election? The three counties with the largest percentage decreases—Howard, Carroll and Shelby—are all predominantly Catholic counties; the first two in fact are among the most heavily Catholic counties in the state. In the five most Catholic counties in Iowa, Culver's percentage decrease was 12.8, much higher than his state average. Calculating the results from all counties where Catholics comprise a plurality, we find that Culver's decrease was 10.2 per cent, still greater than his statewide average. So it appears that Culver lost his support mostly in the Catholic counties. Given the fact that Catholics are not the primary supporters of the New Christian Right, although both Christian Voice and the Moral Majority have Catholics in their memberships, we can conclude that the anti-Culver vote was not primarily the result of the New Christian Right efforts. In fact, the evidence points more clearly to the idea that the anti-Culver vote was an antiabortion vote. It was the Catholics, not the Protestants, who defeated Senator Culver.

This conclusion receives further support from the results of the Des Moines Register exit poll of voters. The newspaper reported that about one-fifth of the voters identified themselves as born-again Christians who agreed with the goals of the Moral Majority. Of this group, "two thirds . . . gave their votes to Reagan and Grassley. But the study indicates this is nothing new in Iowa because the group voted in about the same relative numbers for Republican candidates in 1976 and 1978." The Register concludes: "The study shows clearly that these people failed in their effort to find and register new voters for the 1980 election."[18]

In summary, the evidence we have examined leads to the conclusion that the impact of the New Christian Right on the 1980 election was minimal rather than determinative. Their efforts served to reinforce a trend that would have occurred anyway. For the most part the voters to whom they appealed would have voted for the conservative candidates, and these candidates would have been victorious regardless of the work of Christian Voice and the Moral Majority. Despite the claims of Jerry Falwell, the New Christian Right was just one of many dynamics bringing Ronald Reagan to the Oval Office and a Republican majority to the U.S. Senate.

6
Evangelical Support for the New Christian Right

THE PRESIDENTIAL ELECTION OF 1980 was the first electoral trial for the New Christian Right; the organizations were beginning to grow, the state and local affiliates were just starting, and the leadership was getting its first drink of the political waters. The fact that their efforts in that election were not the most important determinants of the victories and losses does not consign this movement to obscurity, for the potential of an evangelical voting block still exists.[1]

Although both Christian Voice and the Moral Majority seek a broad level of support that crosses religious lines, it was clear from the outset that evangelicals were the primary constituents. In order to assess the future of the movement, therefore, it is crucial to examine the nature and extent of evangelical support for the New Christian Right. For this purpose a mail questionnaire was sent to 272 evangelical pastors in Iowa and South Dakota in early 1981, asking for their evaluations of the New Christian Right movement. Although a two-state survey is not as comprehensive as we might like, the results can illustrate and reinforce some trends available in other studies.

Included in the sample in these two states were Baptists, Lutherans, Methodists and United Presbyterians. The questionnaire sought information about the political activities of the ministers, their awareness of the religious groups, their stances on several policy issues judged important by the New Christian Right and their feelings about the proper role of the clergy in political matters. The total response rate was just under 60 per cent (162 of 272). Among the specific denominations represented, the highest response rates came from the American Baptists (76 per cent), Methodists (66 per cent) and United Presbyterians (64 per cent), while the Missouri Synod Lutherans responded at a disappointing rate of only 37 per cent.

The ministers in the survey confirmed that the New Christian Right had been active in the 1980 election, the Moral Majority far more visibly than Christian Voice. Fifty-one of the respondents said they had been contacted about the Senate race in their state by the Moral Majority, whereas only six had received any contact from Christian Voice. Eleven respondents had been contacted by the state affiliates of the Moral Majority: Iowans for Moral Government (6 contacts) and People Serious about Liberty and Morality (PSALM, 5 contacts).

Evangelical Support

Even though only one-third of the group had been contacted by the Moral Majority, most of the ministers had heard about the group. On the whole, their impressions were not favorable, as table 2 indicates. More than two-thirds had unfavorable impressions while only one-fourth were favorable.

Impressions	Respondents
Very favorable	4.4%
Somewhat favorable	19.6%
Neutral/no opinion	6.9%
Somewhat unfavorable	29.1%
Very unfavorable	39.9%

Table 2. Ministers' Responses to the New Christian Right

These findings become more meaningful when we show the patterns of support by denomination. Table 3 indicates quite dramatically that Baptists are the most supportive, Lutherans, Methodists and Presbyterians being much less so.

Denomination	Favorable	Unfavorable	Neutral
American Baptists	48%	48%	6%
Southern Baptists	50%	50%	—
Lutherans-Missouri Synod	8%	70%	23%
Lutherans-ALC	16%	84%	—
Methodists	12%	86%	3%
United Presbyterians	12%	85%	3%

Table 3. Denominational Support

The Baptist support does not come as much of a surprise because, as we have seen, many of the groups' leaders are Baptists. Furthermore, many Baptists, particularly from the South, tend to be more conservative ideologically and therefore would be more receptive to the appeals of the groups. On the other hand, the mainline Protestant denominations (Methodists and Presbyterians) are generally seen as more liberal in their stances toward policy issues and thus tend more to reject the New Christian Right.

The most surprising observation is that twice as many American Lutherans express support for these groups as do Missouri Synod Lutherans. It is also interesting to note that almost one-fourth of the Missouri Synod Lutherans say they are neutral or have no opinion. This seems to suggest a greater tendency to keep distant from politics, which is a pattern that will find support in other data presented below.[2]

Historically, similar patterns of support and opposition existed for the religious movements led by Carl McIntire and Billy James Hargis.[3] We should also note that, although Baptists are the most supportive to a considerable extent, there is a polarizing tendency within the group: as many of them are negative as are positive in their evaluations. These figures indicate that the New Christian Right may have a selective following even within the groups that on the surface tend to be most supportive.

How strong is the support or opposition? One way to measure it is to see whether the ministers agree or disagree with the policy stances taken by the groups. The questionnaire asked the pastors to indicate their own stance on a dozen of the issues which the New Christian Right has been concerned about. Each respondent was ranked on a scale of zero to twelve depending on the number of times his own position matched that taken by the Moral Majority or Christian Voice.[4]

The findings (see table 4) indicate that these policy-support scores vary among issues. The whole sample is most supportive of the groups' positions on the issues of balancing the federal budget, opposing the use of government funds for welfare abortions and opposing busing as a way to integrate schools. The ministers generally took stances contrary to the New Christian Right on the issues of restoring prayer in the public schools, abolishing the Department of Education, supporting tax credits for parents who send their children to private schools, the antiabortion amendment and increased defense spending. Taking the sample as a whole, there is support for four of the issue positions of the groups, opposition for seven and a nearly even split on the Equal Rights Amendment. The average policy-support score for the ministers was 4.48 on a scale of zero to twelve. In short, the data do not indicate overwhelmingly strong support among the clergy for the policy positions of the groups.

Issue Stance	Agree	Disagree	Other
Defending Taiwan	39%	23%	38%
Prayer in public schools	17%	63%	20%
Department of Education	16%	66%	18%
Busing	58%	27%	15%
Balanced budget	78%	7%	15%
Funding welfare abortions	62%	31%	7%
Defense spending	35%	53%	12%
Abortion amendment	28%	54%	18%
Equal Rights Amendment	45%	45%	10%
Funding day care	25%	49%	26%
Commitment to Israel	27%	40%	33%
Tuition tax credits	23%	56%	20%

Table 4. Ministers Agreeing with NCR Positions

Again, however, we need to divide the ministers by denomination. The pattern we find is consistent with our earlier findings. Table 5 shows higher policy-support scores among those denominations that tend to be the most favorable toward the New Christian Right. The major surprise in table 5 is the higher support scores for the Missouri Synod Lutherans than for American Baptists and ALC Lutherans. However, when we remember the relatively large proportion of Missouri Synod Lutherans who expressed neutralism, and by implication a nonpolitical stance, this disparity may be partially resolved. We should also note that Lutherans as a whole and especially the Missouri Synod Lutherans were the most reluctant to take a policy position on these issues. They were far more likely to indicate that they neither supported nor opposed the preferences listed. Thus it is clear that those who support these religious groups also adopt the appropriate issue stances while those who oppose the groups take different stances.

Denomination	Average Support Score (on a scale of 0 to 12)
Southern Baptists	6.25
Lutherans-Missouri Synod	6.08
American Baptists	5.91
Lutherans-ALC	4.00
United Presbyterians	3.23
Methodists	2.56

Table 5. Policy-Support Scores by Denomination

The implications are interesting. While it is clear that group supporters have higher support scores, it is also apparent that several supporters disagree with the groups' positions on certain issues. Strategically, it may not be wise for the Moral Majority and Christian Voice to push very hard on things like abolishing the Department of Education, instituting tax credits for private-school tuition and establishing prayer in the public schools. Yet these educational issues are very important to the groups; they have been against federal government involvement in private schools and have argued that public schools are havens for secular humanists who are eating away the moral fiber of our society.

Another series of questions asked the ministers to indicate which of the several policy options was closer to the principles found in the Bible. As we have seen, the New Christian Right insists that the Bible speaks clearly to contemporary policy problems in such a way that we can determine a biblical vote on many issues. The majority of the respondents claimed on the majority of the issues that there was not a single biblical position.

The ministers were most likely to see a clear biblical position on abortion, defense spending and the Equal Rights Amendment. However, we must note quickly that even on these issues there was no consensus about which position was the biblical one. For example, the New Christian Right sees a biblical call for more defense spending but only 10 per cent of the respondents agreed; in contrast, 39 per cent saw a biblical mandate for reducing our defense expenditures. The groups also oppose the ERA on biblical grounds, contending that the proper role of women is to be wife and mother. Only 21 per cent of the pastors agreed, while 44 per cent interpreted the Bible as supporting the constitutional amendment.

Denominational differences are also evident in this regard. Baptists are the most likely to see a biblical basis for their issue positions, whereas Lutherans are least likely. Interestingly, the Methodists are almost as likely as the Baptists to base their preferences on biblical principles, but in almost every case they disagreed with the Baptists about what the Bible really says. Generally, the Presbyterians tended to agree with the Methodists; the Lutherans, when they saw a biblical position, agreed more often with the Baptists.

Stepping back to look at the broader picture of support for the New Christian Right, we can see that its appeal strikes home in a narrow segment of American Protestantism and that even within this segment there is some significant opposition. In other words, its base of support is fragile and could easily be undermined by efforts to push on some issues rather than others. On the other hand, however, there is a small

group of supporters who see a biblical basis for supporting
the positions of the New Christian Right on most issues and
who could be mobilized for political action. The crucial
question, then, is whether these people tend to be involved
in politics anyway, even without the mobilizing efforts of the
Moral Majority and Christian Voice. If so, then the groups
will have had only a reinforcing effect in the political arena.
Thus it is important to look more closely at the regular political activities of these pastors.

These ministers were very active in 1980 in comparison
with the average American citizen. Whereas just over 50 per
cent of the eligible public actually voted, well over 90 per
cent of the ministers reported that they had cast a ballot. In
addition, 21 per cent claimed to have contributed money to a
political campaign, almost a quarter had attended a political
meeting or rally and more than two-thirds had urged their
congregations to register and vote. Nor was 1980 an active exception. When asked about their activities in other elections,
the figures were about the same. Once again, it is apparent
that Lutherans were the least likely to become involved;
Methodists and Presbyterians tended to be the most active.

When we look at the election activities and levels of support for the New Christian Right, we see some interesting
patterns. The most fervent supporters *and* the most intense
opponents of the groups seemed to be the most active; the
less intense one's feelings toward the groups, the less likely
that person was to be very active in the election. But in response to a question about whether the groups' appeals motivated them to participate, very few said that the appeals
were important in their decision to take part. Two-thirds
said the appeals were not important at all and another 14
per cent said the appeals were of only minor importance.
Thus it seems as though these ministers would have been
active with or without the efforts of the new groups.

One interesting fact emerges when we look at the 10 per

cent who admitted that the groups' appeals were important motivators to them. As many of these people were opposed to the groups as were supportive. In other words, the data show a negative reaction developing among a small segment of the clergy. Three of the five negatively motivated pastors took the opportunity to explain the nature of their motivations. One said: "The more I read, the more I voted *opposite* of what they asked." Another commented that the appeals "prompted me to take stronger action contra their urgings."

Besides knowing how much support or opposition there is for the New Christian Right, it is useful to understand why the pastors feel as they do. One open-ended question asked them to comment about their impressions of the groups. The opponents were far more explicit in their observations, and their opposition was wide ranging.

There were several reasons for dissatisfaction. The reason most often cited was the legislator-rating scale developed by Christian Voice to assess the "morality" of the candidates. An Iowa Methodist commented: "We do not need a so-called Christian lobby judging the candidates with a fallacious rating system and pretending that their system accurately judges Christianity or morality in voting by candidates." Others expressed more general dissatisfaction with the tactics of the groups; one called it McCarthyism, and another said their practices were "more like Hitler than Christ." Another complaint was the intolerance displayed by the groups. A Southern Baptist argued that "history shows religious groups in power are the most intolerable." Still others thought the groups were too simplistic in their approach to complex policy problems.

Some thought their use of the Bible to derive policy preferences was inappropriate. One Iowa Presbyterian observed: "I do not believe that I or anyone can prove that the Bible supports my position." Another pastor said that "specific positions must always be held with tentativeness and uncertainty as far as biblical endorsement is concerned."

A Methodist minister accused the group of being against civil rights and peace while trying to preserve wealth. Several referred to the groups as a sign of civil religion, including one who said: "It is my opinion that they reflect a super America civil religion that is not only unChristian but anti-Christian." Finally, a couple of ministers commented about the potentially negative impact on the traditional mission of the church; a Lutheran argued that the groups may offend some Christians and be a hindrance to reaching others with the gospel. Although chapter seven will offer a more extensive critique of the New Christian Right from the entire evangelical community, we should note here that these comments from clergy in two states are not untypical.

Even among the groups' supporters there was some reluctance to identify too closely, especially because of the tactics employed. One comment by a Southern Baptist echoed several others: "Some of their views are valid but their cause isn't helped by baptizing right-wing politics into Christianity."

Having examined the nature and level of support for the New Christian Right, we need also to look at the way in which these ministers use their office as an instrument of their political activity. A series of questions concerned the pastors' perceptions of what could properly be done during a worship service and what should be left out of the service. In general the respondents felt they had much greater freedom to talk about political issues outside of the service, although even here only a third thought that it was appropriate to persuade people to vote for specific candidates. Table 6 indicates these perceptions. The data indicate that ministers feel more comfortable with nonpartisan activities such as raising issues and encouraging voter turnout.

In this respect too there are differences among the denominations. As we might expect from the earlier findings, Lu-

Political Activity	Percentage Who Think Activity Is Proper	
	During Worship Service	Outside of Worship Service
Raise issues for information	59%	81%
Urge people to register and to vote	81%	96%
Persuade people to vote for specific candidate	3%	34%
Suggest preferable policy stances	36%	70%

Table 6. Perceptions of Proper Political Activities

therans are less likely to feel that any of these activities might be appropriate for clergy, both within and outside of a worship service. Presbyterians and Methodists tend to be the most active but are still reluctant to persuade people to vote for their own preferred candidate.

Thus, if it is true that the New Christian Right seeks to mobilize ministers who will in turn activate their own congregations, there is a much more active clergy in those denominations that express the least support for the groups. Where support for the New Christian Right is higher, the ministers show a greater reluctance to use their office for political appeals. This is not really surprising when we consider the historical tendency of the more fundamentalist churches to stay away from the political order. The separationist tendencies are deeply ingrained in church tradition, and any significant change in these attitudes will take years to develop.

A final set of questions asked the ministers for their perceptions of the influence of the Moral Majority and Christian Voice on their congregations. The majority of the respondents (61 per cent) felt the groups had little or no influence;

only 15 per cent perceived any significant influence. Baptists were more likely to perceive some influence, but also more likely to admit that they had no basis for making a judgment. If all of these perceptions are accurate, it lends further credibility to the thesis that the New Christian Right was not very successful in mobilizing the evangelical vote in the 1980 elections.

A more extensive study of the attitudes of Southern Baptist pastors was conducted by James Guth of Furman University; the results lend support to the conclusions we have just examined.[5] Relying on a survey of 450 Southern Baptist ministers across the country, Guth found that the respondents were almost evenly split between those who sympathized with the Moral Majority and those who opposed the group. Only 3 per cent were members, another 43 per cent were sympathizers, and 47 per cent expressed opposition. Guth discovered that those who were more sympathetic also tended to be fundamentalist in theology, politically conservative, somewhat less educated and from a lower class or farm background. This polarization of Southern Baptist attitudes suggests that the New Christian Right has a lot of work to do if it wants to appeal to a group that by most accounts should be a natural part of their constituency.

Conclusions

As a result of these studies we can conclude that the New Christian Right does not represent the opinions of the entire evangelical community. Rather its support comes from the smaller fundamentalist parts of American Protestantism. Even within this latter group, support seems to depend on the types of issues that are stressed and especially on the kinds of tactics that are employed. Christian Voice, the more explicitly religious of the two groups, has a greater problem in that ministers are less aware of its existence and its appeals. The Moral Majority, because it seems to be de-emphasizing its religious roots, may be in danger of losing support from fundamentalist pastors who tend to see their religious convictions as the predominant source of their actions. The implications of these and other factors affecting the future of the New Christian Right will be discussed more completely in the last chapter.

7

A
Religious
Critique

HAVING EXAMINED THE BROADER objectives, the specific policy platform and the strategies of the New Christian Right, we turn our attention to the reactions they have generated within their prized constituency, the evangelical community. We saw in the last chapter the attitudes of pastors in two states, but here our concern is with the larger body of evangelicals across the country. For a movement that seeks to mobilize the political power of evangelicals, these groups have certainly evoked a host of negative reactions. In order to understand their potential impact on American politics, therefore, we must examine these criticisms. In addition to my earlier critique,[1] several scholars, pastors and interested citizens have filled the media with incisive, and occasionally bombastic, evaluations.[2] What follows is a summary of the more significant charges leveled against the New Christian Right.

At the outset it is important to note two things. First, it is unfair to criticize the New Christian Right for trying to exercise influence over political affairs. To criticize it for violating the wall of separation between church and state is to miss the important distinction between the actions of an institutional church and the convictions of individual Christians. This movement is calling upon persons, not churches, to use their votes to elect certain candidates. That is a fundamental right without which democracy is threatened. Such criticism also ignores the legitimate role which religious beliefs have almost constantly played in establishing this nation and guiding public policies. Thus we cannot appropriately criticize the New Christian Right for its involvement in politics, nor can we condemn other religious organizations, such as the National Council of Churches, for their earlier actions in support of civil-rights legislation and in opposition to the war in Vietnam. As John Bennett puts it: "Those who disagree with the Moral Majority people should attack the substance of their commitments rather than their right to be political."[3]

Second, it is important to note again that not every person or group within this movement is vulnerable to every attack that is or can be made. As we have indicated, the Moral Majority has been de-emphasizing the biblical roots of its policy prescriptions while concentrating on moral appeals that transcend religious or denominational boundaries. Therefore, criticisms directed against the ideas expressed in Dr. Falwell's book are not automatically applicable to the Moral Majority as an organization. Furthermore, not every new right group has taken a position on every issue, as we noted in chapter three; thus, for example, it is unfair to criticize the Moral Majority for taking wrong stances on South Africa or Taiwan. There simply has been no official Moral Majority statement on these issues, although some of their earlier fund-raising letters alluded to these countries in appealing for a strongly anticommunist defense policy. Those who criticize the New Christian Right have an obligation to avoid leveling broad criticisms at a movement when only certain parts of that movement are involved.

Ideology and the Scriptures

One of the most vehement criticisms of the early Moral Majority and of Christian Voice is the charge that they incorrectly linked biblical principles with political and economic conservatism. In fact, some critics have argued that these groups may perhaps be reading the Scriptures through the lens of their ideology rather than trying to derive specific issue positions from the Bible. Several new right leaders have either stated or strongly implied that one could not be a Christian and a liberal at the same time. The morality report cards of legislative voting records also show this linkage; those legislators who score highest on the groups' morality scales also tend to be those who score highest on ratings compiled by groups such as Americans for Constitutional Action, which is generally seen as one of the more conservative groups which evaluate voting records.

The critics say that it is impossible to subsume the principles of God's revelation neatly under the rubric of a conservative ideology—or a liberal one for that matter, although recently the latter argument has not been particularly visible. They point, for example, to the frequent biblical injunctions to care for the poor and the oppressed. Or they refer to Jesus' statement in Matthew 25 that those who feed the hungry, visit the sick and clothe the naked will inherit the kingdom of heaven. John Bennett confesses his own sense of wonder at how Falwell can ignore these biblical mandates: "How anyone who claims to be thoroughly biblical can be so little impressed by the passion of the prophets for social justice or by the identification of Jesus with the poor and in general with the victims of society is beyond my understanding."[4]

Opponents would call for the New Christian Right to shake
its conservative view that government has at most a small
role in meeting human needs and to accept the responsibility
to pursue justice with every available means, including the
massive resources of government. After all, they would argue, the Bible certainly includes no clear statement prohibiting a governmental role in welfare. The point is that all of
these emphases are noticeably missing in the platform of
the New Christian Right, just as they are missing in the statements of ideological conservatives.

Related to this argument, Falwell goes to great length in
his book to contend that the free enterprise system is consistent with biblical teachings; the implication is strong that
free enterprise might be the only form of economics that
follows from Scriptures. The heart of the free enterprise system is the idea of maximum human freedom, particularly
the freedom to use one's economic resources and talents
without governmental interference. Freedom is crucial to
ideological conservatives.

The critics, however, claim that there must be limits on
individual freedom and that the Bible clearly recognizes
these limits. For one thing, the Bible proposes that property
is ultimately owned by the Creator, not the creature. The
notion that the earth is the Lord's is certainly biblical, but it
is also certainly foreign to the precious rights of private property claimed by conservatives. Other limits on human freedom are portrayed in the Leviticus account of the Year of
Jubilee and in the account of the early church with its practices of sharing. In short, those who attack the New Christian
Right argue that freedom may not be the ultimate value;
rather, many of them suggest that justice and love take prece-
dence when the claims of freedom collide with the needs
of others. Complete economic freedom for individuals and
groups must be tempered with a concern for social justice.

Robert Webber pushes this argument even further to make

an insightful point about the underlying view of human nature expressed by Falwell:

> A second criticism of Falwell's ideology is that it is too optimistic about the nature of humanity. This is evident in his uncritical support of the free enterprise system. Even if a good case can be made for free enterprise, the failure to recognize the misuse and abuse of this system by those who are motivated by greed is a major flaw.[5]

We must put this argument in perspective. It is true that Falwell and other new right preachers accept the view of human nature developed by John Calvin—that humans are by nature sinful creatures, prone to seek their own good and prone to commit evil. But somehow this notion of individual self-love does not get translated into their perspectives on economic systems, for they seem to forget that economic greed too is a sin, just as are adultery, lying and making idols.

The Role of Government

A second line of criticism is that the New Christian Right has an inconsistent view of the proper role of government in society. Nearly everyone within the movement has cried out against excessive government interference in the economy, particularly in the field of education. According to Falwell, it is wrong to use the power of government to promote homosexuality, to legalize abortions on demand, to teach secular humanism to our children in the public schools, or to use the Internal Revenue Service and the Department of Education to require that certain kinds of courses be taught or certain kinds of people be hired under an affirmative action mandate. Yet these groups unanimously call for increasing the budget of the Pentagon and for passing legislation that will prohibit abortions, restrict pornography and drug traffic, and encourage prayer in the public schools. In other words, they scream bloody murder if the secular humanists try to use the power of government for their ends, but they see it as entirely legitimate for their own movement to use that same government to promote and enforce a different brand of morality.

One does not have to be a supporter of secular humanism to see the inconsistency. If it is not right for one group to rely on governmental power to force its lifestyle on another group, so it should also be improper for the latter group to do that very thing itself. Even if we agree that people should follow biblical morality, it does not then follow that we have the exclusive right to direct the enforcement powers of our government. In a pluralistic society made up of people with very different religious and ethical backgrounds, no single group or coalition should be able to enforce a moral standard that is unacceptable to large numbers of people. The more appropriate kind of response would be for these people to persuade their opponents that their cause is right, perhaps even converting them to their religious beliefs. But such actions are not within the preserve of government.

In this respect, some critics view Falwell as the American version of Adolf Hitler or as this country's Ayatollah. Such attacks are unfair; they cruelly exaggerate the intolerance of the New Christian Right and seriously distort the absolutely grim realities of life and death in Nazi Germany and contemporary Iran. These critics must be more sensitive to the significant difference between attempting to legalize a particular pattern of behavior on the one hand and executing those guilty of certain traits or behavior patterns on the other.

According to Falwell the main function of government is to "execute wrath upon those who do evil."[6] Evil comes from two sources: foreign attack and domestic lawlessness. While he therefore proposes a decreasing role for the government in social and economic areas, he calls for a stronger defense and more funds for law enforcement. Critics wonder whether these two sources of evil really exhaust the possibilities. Could evil also encompass raping the land through haphazard industrial, mining and agricultural practices? Would evil also include polluting the air and water, not only in this country but around the world as other nations try to imitate our industrial progress? Is it not also evil for rich people to spend luxuriously for their own desires while scorning the basic survival needs of others? If government is supposed to be an avenger of evil, then perhaps it must also address these clear social and environmental evils. Yet the New Christian Right does not seem to account for the evilness of these activities.

Supernationalism

In addition to decrying the ideological determinism and theoretical inconsistency just discussed, some spokesmen within the evangelical community have reacted to the intense nationalism that underlies much of the New Christian Right's positions on foreign policy. According to these critics, the flag-waving patriotism pervading the "I Love America" rallies borders on idolatry. Linder and Pierard use the term *civil religion* to describe this phenomenon of mixing religion and excessive nationalism.[7] From Falwell's perspective the United States is the major instrument which God will use to evangelize the world and to defeat the communists. Critics respond that respect for the founding fathers because they invoked the name of God does not make the Declaration of Independence and the Constitution a part of the biblical canon, nor does it make these documents but a little lower than the Heidelberg Catechism or the Westminster Confession.

Intense nationalism, the attitude of "my country: love it or leave it," can lead to a militant xenophobia that both enrages the citizens of other countries who have long suffered from the racism of the colonial powers and denies the universality of the body of Christ. To argue that the United States is God's last hope is to ignore the possibility of divine inter-

vention through the actions of other nations and to belittle
the notion of God's sovereignty, which is central to the beliefs of most evangelicals. Those who argue against superna-
tionalism point to Jesus' summary of the law of God; he said
that our first duty was to love God and our second duty was
to love others as we love ourselves. Nowhere in these com-
mands is there a recognition of modern nation states; in fact,
nation states and the ideology of nationalism that attends
them may be responsible for setting up or at least maintaining distinctions between people that violate the second com-
mand noted by Jesus.

In this respect several opponents have attacked the excessive concentration of the New Christian Right on the evils
of communism while it ignores the injustices and oppression
that came with nineteenth-century colonialism and that still
occur with this century's economic imperialism. In this
sense the charge is that the zeal of the groups to preach
against the sins of the communists has blinded them to the
sins of the anticommunist countries in the third world who
systematically imprison, torture and murder their own
people.

There can be no doubt that the movement is concerned
about the dangers posed by the Soviet Union. The call for
strong military forces and for the support of anticommunist
countries around the world has drawn the fire of others in
the evangelical community. Those associated with the publication *Sojourners* have repeatedly spoken of the idolatry
of the arms race; they have emphasized the biblical call to
trust in the Lord rather than in the sword.[8] Following the
call to be peacemakers, these evangelicals have seriously
questioned Falwell's proposition that the United States must
spend considerably more on defense. Even further, his idea
that simply deterring the Soviets is not enough scares some
of the critics; they wonder whether this is not in fact a covert
call for a pre-emptive strike. In short, the critics charge that

the New Christian Right inadequately understands the dangers of military confrontation and exaggerates the military aspects of national power.

Furthermore, Christian Voice and Falwell (although not the Moral Majority in recent months) have called for virtually unconditional U.S. support of anticommunist governments in Taiwan, South Africa and other countries. The argument, as it has also been accepted by the Reagan administration, is that the gravest threat to the world comes from the USSR and that we should do anything we can to help those nations who agree with us in the cold war.

What is missing here, according to the critics, is any recognition that these third-world countries have awful records on maintaining human rights and domestic justice. The New Christian Right seems to ignore, or consider of little importance, the fact that these countries are not democracies in most senses of the term and that many of them are spending precious resources on armaments not to fight or deter the Soviets, but to put down movements within their own countries that threaten the tight hold which current leaders have.

In other words, the critics charge that the New Christian Right places a higher value on anticommunism than on human life and meaningful individual development, a value judgment which they claim finds little support in Scripture or in evangelical theology. The argument is that the new movement has an excessively rigid Manichean view of the world; they too easily see only good and evil (as defined by one's stance in the cold war) without realizing that some of the liberation movements in the third world stem from the struggles over economic development and human dignity rather than from an international communist conspiracy. By seeing communist red everywhere, Falwell oversimplifies the tensions within the developing world and demonstrates an insensitivity to the plight of people who lack the basic necessities for daily survival.

Ignoring Certain Issues

Running through the last several arguments has been the claim that the New Christian Right overemphasizes some issues which the Bible does not directly address while it ignores other issues for which scriptural preferences are abundant. For example, the groups tend to stress freedom rather than justice, yet biblical references to justice greatly outnumber the references to freedom. The legislative report cards of Christian Voice fail to include votes on such issues as food stamps, foreign aid programs or nutrition programs. To be sure, Falwell's church does have an active program of ministering to human needs, but the speakers for the new movement, consistent with their ideology, seek to reduce the role of government in these areas of need. Critics argue that the Old Testament prophets speak directly to government officials when they condemn injustice and that the New Testament passages dealing with the role of government make clear that it has a responsibility to do justice.

A related accusation is that the groups ignore environmental issues when they evaluate candidates and promote new legislation. Despite the centrality of the concept of stewardship in the Scriptures, the new groups are silent about the abuse of creation that has occurred. It may be that their conservative ideology makes them reluctant to propose limits to the economic freedom they espouse so intensely. Or it may be that they have calculated that raising environmental issues would reduce their financial support among the conservative community. Whatever the cause, the silence is noticeable and, according to the critics, unfortunate.

Furthermore, opponents claim that for all the emphasis on the sins of homosexuality, pornography, drugs and abortion, the groups are remarkably shortsighted in pointing to, or even admitting, the sins of greed, racism and sexism. Reading the literature published by the groups, we find no recognition that there may be a history of racial and sexual discrimination in this country. Instead one finds claims that existing affirmative action programs should be eliminated or at least de-emphasized. For a group of people who have been vocal about the rights of unborn children, it is a curious thing to see almost no mention about the rights of minorities. As Richard Neuhaus argues about the Moral Majority, "It is superficial, generally, in its analysis of what is wrong with society. God knows there's a lot that's wrong. But it focuses upon the symptoms of moral degeneracy, condemns them vigorously but its causes, the causes of this degeneracy in a materialistic and individualistic society, are seldom traced."[9]

Political Solutions to Religious Problems
Another charge directed against the groups involves the excessive fascination they have with political solutions to national problems. Robert Webber in particular has argued that the Moral Majority is seeking to address innate human fallibilities through political activities rather than the soul-winning work of the church. Webber contends that Falwell attributes to the nation a task that is properly the responsibility of the church: salvation will not come from passing laws but only from passing the good news of God's grace demonstrated in the death of Jesus. In other words, the Moral Majority errs in looking for earthly political answers to what are ultimately divine prerogatives.[10]

Legislative Report Cards
Finally, some people have reacted negatively to the attempts by Christian Voice to evaluate the morality of a legislator's voting record in Congress. Although, as we saw in chapter four, this is not a new strategy for interest groups, even some of the groups' supporters have cautioned against the implication that those legislators who received low scores were somehow less moral individuals. By now we are aware that

certain congressmen who were rated very high in the evaluations have led rather imperfect lives tainted with homosexuality, drunkenness and corruption. In contrast, other legislators who were rated near the bottom of the scale have been
leaders in the movement to relate their religious convictions
to their legislative choices. We have already noted that some
of the members of the Christian Voice congressional advisory
committee have resigned as a result of the release of these
report cards.

Robert Grant and other leaders of the New Christian Right
have been doing all sorts of backtracking and explaining in
order to justify their report cards, but to little avail. Many
in the evangelical community have expressed doubt that
votes on a dozen issues in Congress are truly indicative either
of a person's individual morality or of fitness for public office. These doubts are further confirmed when we notice
again that votes on several moral issues—hunger, health
care, pollution—were not included in the reports.

The report cards have been especially confusing for evangelical Christians who have access to comparable ratings
compiled by other Christian groups. It is clear that various
Christian groups differ substantially in their evaluations of
particular legislators. Table 7 shows just one example of the
differences: it compares the Christian Voice ratings of several
U.S. senators with the ratings published by Bread for the
World, a group more narrowly concerned with national and
international hunger issues.

On the basis of these comparisons, can Christian voters
say that Senator Helms, for example, is more moral than
Senator Riegle, or that Senator Humphrey deserves more
support than Senator Cranston?

In summary, the critics argue that it is impossible to measure effectively the morality of a legislative voting record on
the basis of a handful of votes in one Congress. What particularly irks these critics is the implication that legislators who

Senator	Christian Voice Rating	Bread for the World Rating
Cranston	0	100
Culver	0	100
McGovern	0	100
Riegle	0	100
Helms	100	0
G. Humphrey	100	0
McClure	92	0
Armstrong	100	14

Table 7. Comparing Ratings of Senators

vote against the self-proclaimed moral position are immoral candidates. This implication was very apparent in some of the New Christian Right efforts in some 1980 congressional campaigns. This kind of negative campaigning—campaigning against one candidate rather than for another—is not new in American politics; but it has reached greater proportions in recent years, and it is a tactic likely to be used by both left and right in future elections.

Positive Contributions
So far we have seen that the New Christian Right does not have the unanimous and enthusiastic support of its evan-

gelical constituency, especially within the mainline Protestant denominations. Yet it would be inaccurate to suggest that it finds no support at all among evangelicals, for several writers have praised the movement for significant and useful aspirations and accomplishments. The rest of the chapter will review this other side of the ledger.[11]

Public opinion polls among the entire public and within the Christian community show a concern with the relaxation of moral standards in this country. No objective observer can deny that social tensions stem from the rising tide of divorce, especially when children are involved; no observer can deny the unhealthy consequences of drug and alcohol abuse; no one can deny the psychological torment and the declining respect for human life when over a million abortions are reported each year. The relationships between the kind of sexual lifestyles portrayed on television and in theaters and the kinds of sexual behaviors among adolescents and adults are probably closer than many free-speech advocates will admit.

Something has happened to the moral fabric of American society, and the evangelical community has responded positively to appeals to think about these social concerns. Despite the fact that some evangelicals may disagree with New Christian Right stands òn abortion and pornography, they do agree that morality must play a more important role as a guide for living. It appears from our analysis of the 1980 election that the New Christian Right has been able to team up with other "moral" movements like the right-to-lifers and the organized opponents of homosexuality. There appears to be a core of support for morality campaigns, and it is clear that some traditionally apathetic citizens have responded in political ways.

At a more fundamental level, some evangelicals are grateful to these groups for demonstrating the moral implications of public policy choices. Prior to the 1980s the evangelical community was rather quiet about politics. Many had avoided political activity completely; others had been active only selectively in fighting against local X-rated theaters or in upholding Sunday closing laws. As a result of the New Christian Right's proclamations, the evangelical community has had a greater opportunity to discover more thoroughly the interrelationships between biblical principles and a whole range of public decisions. The idea that the Bible is relevant to questions about tax policy, for example, or about educational policy, is new to many evangelicals. As some put it, it is about time that the Christian churches realize the full implications of the notion that Jesus Christ is Lord of all, including politics.[12]

Finally, it is clear that many Christians do support many of the specific issue positions of the New Christian Right although, as we noticed earlier, the support is not unanimous. Protestants have generally tended to be very patriotic citizens calling for a strong defense force and active support for our allies abroad. Quite clearly, several million Americans, including vast numbers of evangelicals, are concerned about the increasing power of government. Starting from a firm conviction of human sin, these Christians argue that government, although divinely ordained as an institution, is made up of sinful human beings and therefore is susceptible to being used for the wrong purposes. In short, they are as worried about the abuses of government power as some others are about the abuses of corporate economic power.

In summary, many of the people who are part of the targeted constituency of the New Christian Right are in fact resistant to their appeals. They see the Moral Majority and Christian Voice as intolerant, selective in their biblical interpretations, attuned more to an ideology than to the Scriptures, unfair in their tactics and just plain wrong in some of their issue stances. On the other hand, some in the constituency are fully ready to enter the battle being waged by the groups. As the New Christian Right moves through the Decade of Destiny, they must seek to retain their supporters as well as to persuade their critics. Without the support of large numbers of new political activists, the movement cannot last. The final chapter will trace in more detail the contradictory evidence about whether the New Christian Right will continue to have an impact on American politics.

8
The New Christian Right in the Decade of Destiny

IN EARLIER CHAPTERS WE OBSERVED that the New Christian Right has been able to ride along on a tide of conservative politics since the groups were established in the late 1970s. Even though they were not the most important determinants of the 1980 election results, it would be unfair to write off the Moral Majority and Christian Voice as uninfluential political forces. To assess their potential, we need to look beyond their initial electoral efforts. We need to look, as it were, at the signs of the times. And the signs are mixed. On one hand we see several indicators pointing to a strong role for the New Christian Right in the coming years; on the other, we see some serious obstacles in the road ahead.

Positive Signs
Christian Voice and the Moral Majority have several things

going for them in the short run. Perhaps the most important is the public drift toward conservatism. Mirrored most visibly in the Reagan victory and the stunning Republican takeover of the U.S. Senate, the ideological movement toward the right is also apparent in public opinion polls. Not only are more Americans rebelling against high taxes and governmental interference with their lives, but they are also less likely to identify themselves as liberals and more likely to call themselves moderates and conservatives. Although the New Christian Right is not the cause of this shift, the groups involved can certainly benefit from public dissatisfaction with the liberal policies of the 1960s and their consequences in the 1970s. The secular new right led by Viguerie, Phillips, Weyrich and Dolan appear to be more instrumental in effecting this ideological shift than the Moral Majority or Christian Voice; but to the extent that Falwell and Grant maintain close ties with these leaders, their groups will be able to capitalize on this new-found power. In the short run, at least, conservatives will retain their superiority in mass mailing techniques, which will be crucial for the electoral and legislative battles that lie ahead.

A second positive sign for the New Christian Right is the simultaneous growth of fundamentalist churches in this country. Throughout the 1970s the mainline Protestant churches showed relative declines in membership while the biggest growth took place among the doctrinally strict and evangelistic sects. The growth seems to be particularly concentrated in some of the smaller groups and among independent churches rather than in the larger groupings such as the Southern Baptist Convention. Not only are these fundamentalist churches growing at a faster rate, but there is also abundant evidence that members of these churches are increasingly inclined to see the importance of politics. One clear example is found in the poll commissioned by the Connecticut Mutual Life Insurance Company. It showed that more religious people were 20 per cent more likely to vote in local elections than those who were less religious.[1]

A third reason to expect a continuing strong movement is the obvious mass appeal of groups like the Moral Majority. Growing to a membership of over 4 million within two years is a remarkable feat for any organization. When we realize in addition that the group's followers are scattered in congressional districts all across the country, we can see the possibilities for ready access to many members of Congress. This mass-based nature of the current movement is one of the features distinguishing it from earlier movements directed by people like Carl McIntire. Earlier attempts to link religion and politics simply did not have the popular following and the organizational structure at the grassroots level, both of which are evident with the Moral Majority. The various attempts to establish state and local affiliates or chapters certainly represent a source of strength, for most political analysts agree that elections are won or lost at the local level.

Fourth, the New Christian Right has been blessed by the continuing success of Christian broadcasting and by the initial success of cable television in the United States. By having weekly—sometimes even daily—contact with audiences, the leaders are able to inspire their troops and incite them to regular action. For example, in November 1981 Falwell's "Old Time Gospel Hour" was aired from a small town in Nebraska where local officials had padlocked the doors of a church which had been operating a Christian day school. The school administrators had refused to provide certain information requested by the state, and so the state attempted to close the school. The merits of the action are not crucial here. What we want to note is the ease with which a religious program can be used to make a political point, in this case a point about governmental interference with the rights of citizens to educate their children. The image of church doors chained shut by the government was strong enough for Fal-

well to rouse his supporters and make both a religious and
a political appeal.

Another source of strength for the movement is the diversity of its interests in political issues. It is not a single-
issue group like many we have seen in recent years. What
this means in practice is that groups like the Moral Majority
and Christian Voice can afford to suffer a defeat on one or
two issues because there are dozens of other issues around
which their members can be mobilized. To be sure, some
issues are more important for group survival than others,
but, for example, a congressional defeat of the Human Life
Amendment would simply cause the groups to focus on
another issue. Such a defeat might slow them down a bit or
depress them, but there are other rallying points and other
battles that must be waged. The image of single-issue interest groups in American politics is not a favorable one, and
here the New Christian Right has the advantage of being different. This diversity of interests means that the groups will
have many years of political battle in the 1980s. It is not likely, even considering President Reagan's ability to influence
Congress, that the entire agenda of the New Christian Right
will be brought to a final test in the next two or three years,
so there will be plenty of opportunities for the groups well
into the decade.

One of the greatest reasons for the New Christian Right
to be optimistic about the future is the enthusiasm and ambition of the leadership. Both Grant and Falwell are indeed
extraordinary men filled with visions of what could be accomplished and overflowing with desire to achieve these
dreams. The media publicity surrounding these leaders in
the last few years probably reinforces their ability to attract
followers.

Finally, even the intense and visible opposition to the New
Christian Right serves as a source of strength. Nothing unites
a group so quickly and intensely as the perception of being

persecuted by a common enemy—in this case the liberal news media. Thus when Norman Lear establishes a group called People for the American Way, taking to the airwaves to denounce the inflexibility and intolerance of the Moral Majority, Falwell is even better able to convince the traditionally apathetic fundamentalists that the crucial battle for the soul of the nation has begun. When George McGovern lends his name to a group called Americans for Common Sense, seeking to affect the 1982 elections, it serves to confirm the convictions of New Christian Right supporters that they are right. When the American Civil Liberties Union takes legal action against Falwell and the Moral Majority, conservatives get angry about what they see as a denial of their freedom of speech and assembly. Throughout history there are many examples of groups which claimed to know the truth and were strengthened rather than strangled by the rise of an opposition. Even if most of the media treatment is negative, group leaders can turn that to their profit by portraying themselves as persecuted and misunderstood individuals in danger of losing their right to speak out on the issues.

In short, the New Christian Right has a great potential for impact in American politics because of the overall conservative drift in public opinion, the growth and politicization of fundamentalist churches, the strong appeal to the mass public, its access to the Christian media, the diversity of its appeal, the enthusiasm and ambition of the leadership, and the intensity of the opposition which reinforces its own unity and purpose. In this sense it seems as if the Moral Majority has a brighter future than Christian Voice. The former has greater media access, a more solid grassroots organization, and, with the exception of the Christian Voice legislative report cards, a more vocal opposition. Christian Voice, as a smaller organization with a smaller budget and with a leader who cannot match the national recognition of a Falwell, faces a more uncertain future. If, however, some Moral Majority members become dissatisfied with the reduced religious emphasis of their group, they may switch to Christian Voice as an alternative.

Negative Signs
On the other side of the ledger, several indicators present a less positive future for the movement. For one thing, as we saw in chapter five, there is still a significant antipathy toward politics in evangelical circles. These feelings that politics is a corrupt business and that its importance is secondary to the saving of souls persist among both clergy and laity. It is indeed difficult to transform overnight deeply ingrained attitudes about political participation. We see this most clearly among Missouri Synod Lutherans, who ideologically tend to be sympathetic to the New Christian Right but who largely reject an active political role for pastors and churches.

Furthermore, many of the supporters of the Moral Majority and Christian Voice are political amateurs who have only recently become involved in politics. It is highly likely that such people lack the patience for the incremental changes that can be wrought through the political system. In the best of democratic beliefs they expect a political system to respond immediately to their new direction, and they can become frustrated when the results of their actions seem so marginal. As a result of this frustration, they may adopt a strongly defensive reaction by rejecting future participation in this imperfect vehicle of social change.

It will be difficult for the groups' leaders to maintain the intense interest and concern over the long haul of legislative decision making. The newest converts, for all their initial enthusiasm, may fade into ambivalence and lose the personal drive that is essential for long-term political success. This is even more true to the extent that the movement loses some key congressional battles, as it is bound to do.

Second, the New Christian Right faces an obstacle in view of the fact that its support generally comes from a segment of the American population that is getting smaller as the years go by. The greatest support for the movement comes from people who are less educated, less wealthy and less secular. In contrast, demographic and economic trends seem to indicate that the average American is becoming more educated, more tolerant, wealthier and more secular than his or her parents. Such shifts would suggest that the new movement may be fighting a defensive battle to retain its legitimacy in a society whose values are going in the opposite direction.[2]

The groups also face a threat to their existence precisely because of the rapid growth they have experienced. One of the most important assets which a group can possess is internal cohesion. Such cohesion usually is inversely related to size: the larger a group grows the greater difficulty there is in getting all the members to agree. Both groups have members from various denominations; in one sense this is an asset. But such a strength can quickly turn into a glaring weakness when the members cannot agree on common lists of goals and priorities.

The Catholic supporters, for example, may be most concerned about abortion and government regulation of private schools. Many others may see these issues—especially the latter—as secondary to issues of homosexuality, the economy or American military strength. Because their resources are limited, the groups will have to decide where to concentrate their efforts. In such a situation the competing priorities within the groups will surface and force the leaders to spend more time on achieving intragroup consensus rather than political or legislative impact.

From all appearances, it seems that the Moral Majority runs this risk to a greater extent than Christian Voice. While the latter has continued its strong appeal specifically to fundamentalists, the Moral Majority no longer calls itself a religious organization. It seeks instead to unite all "moral" people whether they be Christians, Jews, Muslims or even atheists. Trying to appeal to such a large group may alienate some of the charter members who joined with Falwell for religious reasons. In the flush of excitement surrounding the 1980 and 1982 elections where the issues were more clearly cut, the potential for internal disharmony was minimized. But when the struggle turns to the slow-moving legislative arena with its multiplicity of committees marking up numbers of bills simultaneously, any disunity may be magnified.

Related to this is the possibility that the informal alliance between the New Christian Right and the secular new right may break down in the process of legislative combat. To be sure, the new right leaders loudly promise their support for the social and moral agenda of the Moral Majority *after* the major economic and defense decisions have been resolved. But what if the latter issues never get resolved to their satisfaction, as seems likely with our current economic woes? What if secular conservatives continue to procrastinate on the social issues, hoping that the New Christian Right will patiently and faithfully support their priorities? Or what if the Reagan administration and the conservative wing of the Republican Party use up all of their bargaining chips on budget and military issues so that by the time Congress debates abortion and school prayer the leverage for making deals is expended?

Such scenarios must haunt Falwell and Grant as they wonder whether their groups are being used for the purposes of the conservatives. There is some reason to question the president's commitment to many of the issues that are so dear to the hearts of Christian Voice and the Moral Majority. President Reagan has admitted that his first concerns are a strong economy and a strong defense. It is likely that these will be continuing battles that will endure throughout his term of office, and it is clear from past history of presidential lobbying in Congress that even the most effective president must refrain from going to the well for support too often.

In this respect, it may be significant that President Reagan has not turned to the New Christian Right in filling the hundreds of administrative vacancies that greet every new administration. The most direct tie between the religious groups and the Reagan administration was the appointment of Robert Billings, a former leader of the Moral Majority, to a high-level position in the Department of Education. Yet this is one of two cabinet agencies that Reagan has proposed to eliminate, and it is obvious that top people in such departments do not enjoy regular access to the Oval Office. Many of the closest advisors to the president were not enthusiastically supported by the New Christian Right. In fact, many of these appointments were bitter disappointments for a movement that perceived its electoral role to be a crucial component of the conservative victory. Just as the born-again crowd left the Carter fold following what they felt to be distinct snubs from the White House, so they may also distance themselves from Reagan as he delays on their priority issues.

Another obstacle to their success is the feeling among the American public, as well as within the administration, that economic issues are more important than social and moral ones. Although members of Christian Voice and the Moral Majority may see the priority of decisions on abortion, school prayer and pornography, it is not clear that the larger public agrees. In fact, public opinion polls which ask citizens to indicate the issues that concern them the most consistently show that pocketbook issues—inflation and unemployment —are the most important. For example, a Gallup Poll taken in late 1981 demonstrated that 52 per cent of the respondents cited the high cost of living as the most important problem facing the nation, that another 17 per cent focused on unemployment, and that only a scant 4 per cent were most concerned with the moral decline in society.[3] Until these economic problems are alleviated, it will be difficult for the New Christian Right to mobilize a coalition to press ahead on other issues. In the light of the economic forecasts coming from the Congressional Budget Office and even the Reagan administration itself, it will be some time before these primary economic anxieties subside.

Both Christian Voice and the Moral Majority have also run into some financial binds if their urgent fund raising letters are any indication. Falwell and Grant have both predicted the collapse of important lobbying and publicity efforts if additional money does not come in quickly. Two factors seem to be problems. One is that both organizations are officially independent from major denominations and therefore often compete with religious groups for scarce resources. This is especially true in rough economic times. Second, contributions to both organizations are not tax deductible because of their political lobbying. Whatever the marvels of modern-day mass mailing, it is still easier to generate revenues when there is an attendant tax break. This too is particularly applicable during a recession. Considering the overall scarcity of financial resources and the residual antipolitical tendencies of many fundamentalists, the possibility exists for continuing fund-raising crises among the New Christian Right.

Finally, the movement's very success in mass mailing and negative campaigns will certainly provoke liberal groups to adopt these techniques in coming elections. It is true that the 1980 election caught the liberals napping, and it is true that Viguerie's mailing list still far surpasses anything put together by liberal organizations; but the gap may be closing. If the 1982 congressional elections are any indication, liberal organizations are learning the tactics and accumulating lists of contributors that will reduce the conservative monopoly in this area. If NCPAC was successful in 1980 because it could legally set up an independent campaign unrestricted by any expenditure ceiling, so too could a series of liberal groups conduct similar campaigns in 1982.

In summary, there are a number of obstacles in the pathway of the New Christian Right as it faces the rest of the 1980s: fundamentalist perceptions of politics as something to avoid, diminishing numbers of the kinds of people who might support the groups, internal differences, cracks in the ties to the political new right, uncertainties about the Reagan administration's commitment to its social agenda, popular concerns with economics rather than morality, finances and stronger opposition from liberals. So the future holds mixed prospects for Christian Voice and the Moral Majority. On the basis of the signs we have discussed, it is reasonably certain that the New Christian Right will be an active, vocal and visible political force well into the decade.

Saying that, however, does not necessarily mean that they will be an influential political force. Several unknowns could affect their impact. For one thing an examination of earlier political-religious groups suggests that they tend to be more effective in times of economic prosperity. In such situations people are not as concerned about pragmatic pocketbook issues and might be more willing to spend time on social issues. However, in an economic crunch popular attention focuses on how to make enough money to feed the family and pay the rent. Social and moral issues are placed on the back burner.

Any major foreign crisis would also turn national attention away from legislative politics as the people rally around the leadership of the president. Such an event would reduce the impact of the New Christian Right. Even though both groups do have distinct foreign policy preferences, these groups would not be perceived as particularly relevant reference points for conducting foreign policy. In Washington politics those groups which would be most directly affected by a policy decision are seen as more legitimate participants in the policy process. The New Christian Right would lack such legitimacy.

Mixing Religion and Politics

The New Christian Right is the most recent manifestation of a long history of attempts to bring religious convictions to bear on American public policy. From the early days of the republic, through the slavery and prohibition debates, to the anticommunism of the cold war, religious people have tried to shape government decisions according to the mold of biblical principles. Every act of this constant drama has witnessed the intensity, frustration and explosiveness which comes from blending pluralistic democracy with theological certainty. The remaining pages seek to outline the difficulties of mixing religion and politics and to offer a few observations about how these difficulties might be minimized.

The greatest difficulty lies in this: a democracy prides itself in its ability to represent a multiplicity of views, achieving a rough and perhaps temporary consensus through periodic elections and official responsiveness to the views of the public. In contrast, religious convictions tend to be more permanent and less open to compromise. After all, say the preachers, the Word of God is clear; our biblical studies convince us that certain behaviors are sinful and thus completely unacceptable. Whether those actions are public or private, it is felt that the church (both clergy and laity) must denounce those sins and call people to a new way of life. The guidelines are clear, enforceable and universal.

In the light of these convictions, how is compromise possible when some groups in society do not adhere to these biblical principles? How can the religious people coexist with those whose behavior is seen as leading them to eternal death? The biblical mandate for witnessing and for seeking conversions is most obvious. So Christians try to do everything they can, including the legislation of personal morality, if necessary, to change the sinful lifestyles of others.

From the perspective of the nonreligious people, though, values are ultimately relative. There is no single, constant, clear set of guidelines by which all people should live. How then can one group—which may or may not include the majority of the population—expect everyone in the society to follow a set of guidelines which others simply do not accept? Does not democracy mean that each group is entitled to fight for its own beliefs and that compromise is necessary to achieve consensus? In short, the struggle pits those who know the truth and feel driven to spread it against those who believe more in a process of governing than in the specific content of its decisions. The dilemma is inherent within a democratic political system and achieves its most visible expression when the government makes or refuses to make decisions about lifestyle.

Another difficulty comes from the fact that churches and denominations have been badly split because of their involvement in political affairs. In the first place, not all members agree that political action is a way of doing God's will. They would prefer to spend limited time and resources saving the lost sheep rather than lobbying Congress or soliciting votes in an election. These people see politics as a diversion from the more important work the church is called to do. So they resist making denominational statements about political issues, or they leave those churches they see entrapped by the worldly powers.

Second, within churches not all people are in agreement about which political option is the most biblical. We have seen in the area of defense policy, for example, that some proclaim biblical support for increased military spending to deter the godless communists while others point to a scriptural mandate for disarmament and pacifism. When church synods or assemblies convene, these different perspectives have led to perceptions that those with different opinions are just not reading the Bible carefully enough. Such feelings can soon transcend the level of political disagreements and reach the level of personal antagonism when one side begins to question the spiritual integrity of the others.

What much of this boils down to is the question of whether political tolerance is compatible with religious conviction. As we have seen, one of the most frequently expressed criticisms of the New Christian Right is the charge that it seeks to impose its brand of morality on everyone in society. Should it be able to use the full force of government power to accomplish these ends? Members of the New Christian Right contend that they are now being forced by the government to tolerate or even accept lifestyles which they find fundamentally abhorrent. Is it legitimate for either group to be able to use the power of government to achieve its objectives when the competing objectives seem ultimately incompatible? These are the questions raised anew with the emergence of the New Christian Right; these are the fundamental questions with which Americans must struggle as they pass through the Decade of Destiny.

In seeking to answer these questions it will be helpful to look at some responses that are not satisfactory. One such response calls for us to separate life into the sacred and the secular, into the religious and the political, into the moral and the morally neutral. In doing so we can assign the church ultimate sovereignty over the former sphere while saving the latter for the government. For example, some might argue that homosexuality is a moral issue and, as such, regulation should fall within the proper sphere of the church, not the state. Others would say that financing public schools is a political question and therefore the church must keep out of the issue.

This distinction, this wall of separation, is an inadequate resolution of the problem for a number of reasons. First, it will inevitably produce all sorts of arguments about where the line actually falls. One could say, for instance, that the issue of homosexuality is a political issue if the government tries to preserve the civil rights of homosexuals. Or one could even claim that it is a political issue if the government does nothing, for by doing nothing the government would in effect be supporting the activities of those who wish to discriminate against homosexuals. Even a government nondecision is really a show of support for the status quo and therefore can be called a moral act.

Second, some people might contend that any argument about where to draw the line is essentially futile because no such line or division exists. For them one's religious convictions form a world and life view that affects every segment of life. Every government decision, no matter how trivial, is in fact a moral decision because it distributes benefits to some and levies costs on others. Even such a simple decision as setting up a bipartisan study commission presupposes some underlying conviction that one state of affairs is preferable to or worse than another. Or, citing the school-financing issue, they would argue that a moral choice is involved in whatever decision is made because it may affect the ability of some schools to educate their students effectively. Many, if not all, fundamentalists would hold fast to the idea that all of life is a moral and religious concern so that it is impossible to delineate a secular sector and a religious sector.

Another unsatisfactory attempt to resolve the dilemma of religion and politics is for the Christian to withdraw from politics. There are a number of sects and denominations which have in effect chosen this alternative. They interpret scriptural passages about the government in the strictest sense, calling only for obedience to public law and payment of taxes. Beyond that, there is no good reason to vote, to write a letter to an elected official or to express support for or opposition to any government decision. This option is inadequate because at its heart is still the notion that there is a clear line between religion and politics. This perspective fails to understand that government decisions are inherently moral and that by avoiding political involvement these people are really supporting what may be immoral actions. Within the confines of one's religious convictions, one cannot be truly neutral toward public policy, for noninvolvement is a sign of support for what the government is doing. One of the greatest contributions of the New Christian Right is precisely this realization that the actions of governing authorities do express a standard of right and wrong. In other words, they are moral acts.

Equally insufficient is the alternative which calls for an end to democracy and the establishment of some sort of authoritarian theocracy ruled subultimately by the clergy. Many liberals fear that this is the final objective of the New Christian Right, despite the Moral Majority's expressions of support for pluralism. Such an option would not and could not work. The United States is simply too heterogeneous in many different ways for 230 million people to agree on a common set of divine mandates, even if all believed in a divine being. The Iran ruled by Ayatollah Khomeini visibly demonstrates the problems such regimes have. That particular government has been held together not so much by agreement on a set of religious principles as by the perceived threat of a common enemy. Such unity is artificial and temporary. Furthermore, ministers do not have the political and managerial skills necessary to run a country.

What then can we do in such a situation? One group claims to know the truth not only for itself but for the entire society, while other groups are equally committed to different perceptions of the truth and resistant to forced conversion through governmental decree? How can we effectively and peacefully mix deeply felt religious convictions with the political realities of a pluralistic society? A complete answer to these questions is beyond the scope of this book, but I will offer a few suggestions.

First, the people in the New Christian Right must realize that their inflexibility is inappropriate. The inflexibility stems largely from their beliefs that the Bible speaks clearly to modern problems, that their interpretation of the Bible is the only correct one and that they have correctly analyzed policy decisions and policy options. It is possible, however, to argue against these attitudes without being unbiblical. That is to say, we can use their own interpretation of the Bible to demonstrate that they should be more flexible.

In a short but perceptive book written in the early 1970s, Paul Henry asks Christians to be a little less sure that they have the single correct interpretation of God's will. Henry presents three reasons for a greater awareness of moral ambiguity.[4] First, he contends that because of the fall of man into sin—a contention that must certainly find agreement within the New Christian Right, we are unable to understand perfectly what the will of God is. Our sin affects our reading of the Scriptures so that our application of its meaning for modern policy problems is imprecise. Second, Henry claims that sinful human beings are also unable to understand completely the factual details of current policy choices. For example, we do not know exactly how many nuclear weapons it takes to deter a Soviet attack, nor do we know the best way to stop criminals from committing crimes. As to the world food crisis, we have a fairly clear idea about how many malnourished people there are, but we do not agree much about whether it is essentially a problem of total food supply or a problem of inadequate distribution. Finally, Henry argues that we must be more flexible because we also have an imperfect understanding of the consequences of political actions. For example, we do not know what would happen to

the crime rate if we approved the death penalty; the studies
that have been done provide ambivalent conclusions. And
we are equally uncertain about what would happen if Congress passed the Human Life Amendment. We have only the
most tentative ideas about how the Soviets would react if
we were to retake control of the Panama Canal, reimpose
economic sanctions on Zimbabwe or sell more weapons to
Taiwan. Because of all these uncertainties, Henry concludes:

> If Christians are to rise above political naiveté, they must
> begin by recognizing that political problems are immense-
> ly complex and clouded. And they must recognize that
> the motives behind political action are generally mixed.
> Hence, politics is not a simple battle between good and
> evil, or virtuous men and evil men.[5]

Following from these ideas, the New Christian Right must
do three things. One is to realize that the Bible, although
clearly concrete about the way of salvation, does not specifically address many of the policy problems we face today.
The Bible does not mention the Panama Canal Treaty or
Russian communism. This is not to say that the Bible has
no relevance for modern policy issues. Rather, it says that
the Bible presents general principles against which fallible
individuals can imperfectly measure contemporary policy
options.

Second, the New Christian Right must sharpen its feeble
attempts at policy analysis. Several sophisticated techniques
to analyze policy options have been developed by social
scientists over the last few decades, and the leaders of Christian Voice and the Moral Majority would do well to utilize
these tools. Much of their current policy advocacy rests on
an inadequate understanding of the complex decisions
which governments make. The present analytical weakness
is easily understood when we realize that most of the New
Christian Right leadership was trained in biblical analysis
rather than policy analysis. Few seminaries in any denomi-

nation develop in their students the skills to understand contemporary society or political and economic choices. Before anyone should attempt to apply biblical principles to specific policy choices, he or she must first understand the causes of the policy problem and the consequences of the alternative solutions. God can also reveal his will through the appropriate use of policy analytic tools.

Third, the New Christian Right most of all must practice more humility in political confrontation. The essence of humility is the belief that one's perceptions may be inaccurate and the willingness to listen to and learn from others whose ideas are different. Humility seeks to reduce the abrasiveness that hinders effective discussions and informed decisions. Humility does not mean an unwillingness to take a strong stand on an issue; rather it means that one's stand is subject to change with the discovery of new evidence or with the emergence of new insights into the nature of the policy problem itself or into the meaning of our normative standards.

Critics of the New Christian Right, however, also need some counsel. Their unwillingness to allow Christian Voice and the Moral Majority to proclaim a biblical position on current issues stands in sharp contrast to their joyous affirmation of the more liberal churches when they called, on biblical grounds, for an end to the war in Vietnam and racial discrimination. It is sheer hypocrisy to deny one group the opportunity to relate the Bible to political issues while praising others for doing that very thing, albeit with different results. We must either allow any group to propose such ideas (which is the preferable choice), or deny that opportunity to all.

The critics must realize too that the objectives and the statements of the New Christian Right do not violate the constitutional separation of church and state. The founding fathers never intended to deny the influence of religious beliefs on political actions. They were instead trying to support religious diversity by guarding against the establishment of an official state church. The distinction between an established church and a set of religious convictions is crucial. The New Christian Right is seeking to bring its religious convictions to bear on what the government does; it is not attempting to set up a national church. It is seeking governmental recognition of and support for a particular set of values; it is not seeking homogeneity of opinion. The particular segment of the evangelical community that forms the backbone of the movement is deeply committed to the separation of church and state which opponents argue they are trying to destroy.

Mutual tolerance is far easier to preach than to practice. It requires an intense commitment to the pluralism which is rather superficially voiced by both sides. What is needed is a deep understanding of the concept of political justice, biblical and otherwise. Political justice legitimates the expression of a multiplicity of views which may or may not be compatible. It seeks government policies that uphold the rights of any minority—racial, religious or ideological—to survive and to act politically. The New Christian Right must not deny anyone the right to live according to a different set of moral guidelines so long as they do not threaten society itself with moral collapse. In like manner, the critics of the New Christian Right must refrain from seeking public policies which would infringe on the rights of fundamentalist Christians to live as they interpret the will of God.[6]

If the conflict about mixing the cross and the flag is essentially a conflict of values, then perhaps the most effective way for the New Christian Right to achieve its objectives is not by passing legislation which will force others to change their lifestyles, but by directing their energies toward the evangelization efforts of local churches. Political action is unlikely to win many converts to the beliefs of fundamentalists; in fact, as we have seen, it frequently serves to rigidify the outsiders. Perhaps the best avenue to personal conversion is the mission outreach of the church. This is not so much drawing a line between the sacred and the secular as it is saying that the church is the more useful instrument for accomplishing certain things and the government for accomplishing others.

Some disagreements cannot be solved through political action. What many liberals have failed to understand is that government is not the only institution in society through which conflicts can be resolved. The church, the family, the corporation and other social groups are legitimate and useful institutions that may effectively settle some societal conflicts.

Unfortunately, the New Christian Right seems to have adopted the liberal view, focusing its efforts on political solutions to value conflicts. Political action, centered as it is in the need for compromise, may offer an insufficient solution to questions about ultimate values. Political remedies, superficial and fleeting as they inherently are, will not correct fundamental social ills.

Politics is useful, it is important, but it is also limited. It is a tool which can be used when there is some common agreement about how to proceed; it is least effective in dealing with conflicting objectives. The New Christian Right cannot achieve its objectives only through politics because its aim is conversion of society. In the same way, however, the opponents of the New Christian Right cannot achieve their objectives by restricting entry to the political arena, because moral standards transcend that arena. In short, the New Christian Right teaches us a lesson we should have learned from the struggles over slavery and prohibition: political action, by itself, is inadequate for solving the fundamental problems of human society.

Notes

Chapter 1: Religion and Politics in the 1980s

[1]"New Right Tops 1980 Religion News," *Christian Century* 97, no. 43 (31 December 1980):1283.

[2]Moral Majority, "Fighting for a Moral America in This Decade of Destiny" (pamphlet distributed in 1980).

[3]Ibid.

[4]"An Interview with the Lone Ranger of American Fundamentalism," *Christianity Today* 25, no. 15 (4 September 1981):24.

Chapter 2: The Roots of the New Christian Right

[1]This and following quotes are taken from the majority opinion in *Roe* v. *Wade*, 410 U.S. 113 (1973).

[2]Kevin P. Phillips, *The Emerging Republican Majority* (Garden City, N.Y.: Doubleday & Company, 1970), chapter 3.

[3]Erling Jorstad, *The Politics of Moralism* (Minneapolis: Augsburg Publishing House, 1981) provides a detailed look at the television church, focusing on the most important preachers and showing how they are interrelated.

[4]*Engle* v. *Vitale*, 370 U.S. 421 (1962).

[5]*Abington School District* v. *Schempp*, 374 U.S. 203 (1963).

[6]For an extended discussion of secular humanism from the perspective of a leader in the New Christian Right see Tim LaHaye, *The Battle for the Mind* (Old Tappan, N.J.: Fleming H. Revell Co., 1980).

[7]George Marsden, *Fundamentalism and American Culture* (New York: Oxford

Univ. Press, 1980).

[8]The roots of the movement and its political efforts are documented in Jorstad, *Politics of Moralism*, and Gary K. Clabaugh, *Thunder on the Right: The Protestant Fundamentalists* (Chicago: Nelson-Hall Co., 1974).

[9]Clabaugh, *Thunder on the Right*, p. xvii.

Chapter 3: The Political Platform of the New Christian Right

[1]"An Interview with the Lone Ranger of American Fundamentalism," *Christianity Today* 25, no. 15 (4 September 1981):1099.

[2]Jerry Falwell, *Listen, America!* (Garden City, N.Y.: Doubleday & Company, 1980), pp. 19-20.

[3]Ibid., p. 244.

[4]Ibid., p. 13.

[5]Ibid., p. 69.

[6]We should note here that one of the criticisms made of the groups is that they are inconsistent in their view of government. The inconsistency comes when they rule out government involvement in the areas cited but call for the government to pass and enforce laws maintaining their version of morality.

[7]Falwell, *Listen, America!* p. 65.

[8]Ibid., p. 85.

[9]Ibid., p. 107.

[10]Ibid., p. 77.

[11]Ibid., p. 181.

Chapter 4: The Politics of Interest Groups

[1]Much of the following analysis relies on ideas expressed in L. Harmon Zeigler and G. Wayne Peak, *Interest Groups in American Society*, 2nd ed. (Englewood Cliffs, N.J.: Prentice-Hall, 1972), especially chapters 1, 3 and 10.

[2]Note that in a few cases the rewards are rather narrowly focused: preserving maximum freedom for private schools, tuition tax credits and gun control. However, the vast majority of their appeals involve intangible or symbolic benefits for an entire society.

[3]Richard Hofstadter, "Pseudo-Conservatism Revisited," in Daniel Bell, *The Radical Right* (Garden City, N.Y.: Anchor Books, 1964).

[4]As one example of this theory, see James David Fairbanks, "The Evangelical Right: Beginnings of Another Symbolic Crusade" (paper presented to the American Political Science Association, New York, September 5, 1981). The notion that the New Christian Right is a cultural defense movement is articulated in James L. Guth, "The Politics of the 'Evangelical Right': An Interpretive Essay" (paper presented to the American Political Science Association, New York, September 5, 1981).

[5]Fairbanks, "Evangelical Right," p. 3.

[6]See John W. Kingdon, *Congressmen's Voting Decisions* (New York: Harper & Row, 1973), p. 56.

[7]Reported in the *Des Moines Register*, 7 September 1980, p. 4A.

Chapter 5: The First Test: The 1980 Elections

[1]Quoted in "Anatomy of a Landslide," *Time*, 17 November 1980, p. 31.

[2]Quoted in "New Resolve by the New Right," *Time*, 8 December 1980, p. 27.

[3]These data come from the *New York Times*/CBS News election day survey, reported in *New York Times*, 9 November 1980, p. A28.

[4]Everett Carll Ladd, "The Brittle Mandate: Electoral Dealignment and the 1980 Presidential Election," *Political Science Quarterly* 96, no. 1 (1981):18.

[5]Ibid.

[6]Seymour Martin Lipset and Earl Raab, "The Election and the Evangelicals," *Commentary* 71 (March 1981):29.

[7]Jim Castelli, "The Religious Vote," *Commonweal* 107, no. 21 (21 November 1980):651.

[8]As reported in Rowland Evans and Robert Novak, *The Reagan Revolution* (New York: E.P. Dutton, 1981), p. 215.

[9]Reported in "New Resolve by the New Right," p. 24.

[10]Reported in Ladd, "Brittle Mandate," p. 7.

[11]*New York Times*, 9 November 1980, p. A28.

[12]Lipset and Raab, "Election and the Evangelicals," p. 30.

[13]"Facts That Help Put Election in Focus," *U.S. News and World Report*, 17 November 1980, p. 39.

[14]See Albert D. Cover and David R. Mayhew, "Congressional Dynamics and the Decline of Competitive Congressional Elections," in Lawrence C. Dodd and Bruce I. Oppenheimer, eds., *Congress Reconsidered*, 2nd ed. (Washington, D.C.: Congressional Quarterly Press, 1981).

[15]Quoted in "New Resolve by the New Right," p. 24.

[16]Lipset and Raab, "Election and the Evangelicals," p. 29.

[17]Erling Jorstad, *The Politics of Moralism* (Minneapolis: Augsburg Publishing House, 1981), p. 97.

[18]*Des Moines Register*, 6 November 1980, p. 4A.

Chapter 6: Evangelical Support for the New Christian Right

[1]This chapter is a revised version of a paper I delivered at the 1981 Annual Meeting of the American Political Science Association, New York, September 5, 1981.

[2]This supports the conclusions about Lutherans presented in Albert J. Menendez, *Religion at the Polls* (Philadelphia: Westminster Press, 1970), chapter 9.

[3]See Richard E. Morgan, *The Politics of Religious Conflict: Church and State in America* (New York: Pegasus, 1968); and Gary K. Clabaugh, *Thunder on the Right: The Protestant Fundamentalists* (Chicago: Nelson-Hall Co., 1974).

[4]One caveat, as we have seen, is that not all of the groups have taken explicit positions on each of these issues; so this measurement is based on a composite picture.

[5]The following observations are drawn from James L. Guth, "The Southern Baptist Clergy: Vanguard of the Evangelical Right?" (paper presented to the Southern Political Science Association, Memphis, Tennessee, November 6, 1981).

Chapter 7: A Religious Critique

[1]Robert Zwier and Richard Smith, "Christian Politics and the New Right," *Christian Century* 97, no. 31 (8 October 1980):937-41.

[2]Note in particular the following useful evaluations from within the evangelical community: Robert E. Webber, *The Moral Majority: Right or Wrong?* (Westchester, Ill.: Cornerstone Books, 1981); Richard Mouw, "Assessing the Moral Majority," *Reformed Journal* 31, no. 6 (June 1981):13-15; and John C. Bennett, "Assessing the Concerns of the Religious Right," *Christian Century* 97, no. 32 (14 October 1981): 1018-22.

[3]Bennett, "Assessing the Concerns," p. 1019.

[4]Ibid., p. 1021.

[5]Webber, *Moral Majority*, p. 31.

[6]Falwell, *Listen, America!* (Garden City, N.Y.: Doubleday & Company, 1980), p. 98.

[7]Robert D. Linder and Richard V. Pierard, *Twilight of the Saints: Biblical Christianity and Civil Religion in America* (Downers Grove, Ill.: InterVarsity Press, 1978).

[8]See, for example, "New Abolitionist Covenant," *Sojourners* 10, no. 8 (August 1981):18-19.

[9]Richard Neuhaus, "The Moral Majority: Threat or Challenge?" (aired 17 May 1981) National Broadcasting Company in association with the United States Catholic Conference, copyright by NBC 1981, transcript, p. 13.

[10]Webber, *Moral Majority*, chapter 12.

[11]In this respect, note that Webber, *Moral Majority*, and Mouw, "Assessing the Moral Majority," both indicate that they appreciate some elements of the groups' appeals.

[12]Mouw, "Assessing the Moral Majority," p. 15.

Chapter 8: The New Christian Right in the Decade of Destiny

[1]Research & Forecasts, Inc., *American Values in the 1980's: The Impact of Belief* (New York: Research & Forecasts, 1981).

[2]See, for example, the argument raised by James David Fairbanks, "The Evangelical Right: Beginnings of Another Symbolic Crusade" (paper presented to the American Political Science Association, New York, September 5, 1981).

[3]As reported in the *Des Moines Register*, 21 October 1981, p. 2C.

[4]These arguments are drawn from Paul Henry, *Politics for Evangelicals* (Valley Forge, Pa.: Judson Press, 1974), pp. 72-79.

[5]Ibid., p. 78.

[6]An excellent and provocative discussion of morality and politics is Lewis B. Smedes, "Cleaning Up the Nation: Nine Theses on Politics and Morality," *Reformed Journal* 30, no. 6 (June 1980):10-13.

Selected Reading List

Books

Bell, Daniel. *The Radical Right*. Garden City, N.Y.: Anchor Books, 1964.

Billings, William. *The Christian's Political Action Manual*. Washington, D.C.: National Christian Action Coalition, 1980.

Clabaugh, Gary K. *Thunder on the Right: The Protestant Fundamentalists*. Chicago: Nelson-Hall, 1974.

Cotham, Perry C. *Politics, Americanism, and Christianity*. Grand Rapids: Baker Book House, 1976.

Crawford, Alan. *Thunder on the Right: The "New Right" and the Politics of Resentment*. New York: Pantheon, 1980.

Falwell, Jerry. *Listen, America!* Garden City, N.Y.: Doubleday & Company, 1980.

Falwell, Jerry, ed., with Ed Dobson and Ed Hindson. *The Fundamentalist Phenomenon: The Resurgence of Conservative Christianity*. Garden City, N.Y.: Doubleday & Company, 1981.

Jorstad, Erling. *The Politics of Doomsday: Fundamentalists of the Far Right*. Nashville: Abingdon, 1970.

――――――――――. *The Politics of Moralism: The New Christian Right in American Life*. Minneapolis: Augsburg Publishing House, 1981.

LaHaye, Tim. *The Battle for the Mind*. Old Tappan, N.J.: Fleming H. Revell Co., 1980.

Linder, Robert D. and Pierard, Richard V. *Twilight of the Saints: Biblical Christianity and Civil Religion in America*. Downers Grove, Ill.: InterVarsity Press, 1978.

Marsden, George. *Fundamentalism and American Culture*. New York: Oxford University Press, 1980.

Menendez, Albert J. *Religion at the Polls*. Philadelphia: Westminster Press, 1970.

Morgan, Richard E. *The Politics of Religious Conflict: Church and State in America*. New York: Pegasus, 1968.

Shriver, Peggy L. *The Bible Vote: Religion and the New Right*. New York: The Pilgrim Press, 1981.

Strober, Gerald and Tomsczak, Ruth. *Jerry Falwell: Aflame for God*. Nashville: Thomas Nelson, 1979.

Viguerie, Richard A. *The New Right: We're Ready to Lead*. Falls Church, Va.: The Viguerie Co., 1980.

Webber, Robert E. *The Moral Majority: Right or Wrong?* Westchester, Ill.: Cornerstone Books, 1981.

Articles

"An Interview with the Lone Ranger of American Fundamentalism." *Christianity Today*, 4 September 1981, pp. 22-27.

Bennett, John C. "Assessing the Concerns of the Religious Right." *Christian Century*, 14 October 1981, pp. 1018-22.

Brown, Robert McAfee. "Listen, Jerry Falwell! A Response to *Listen, America!*" *Christianity and Crisis*, 22 December 1980, pp. 360-64.

Castelli, Jim. "The Religious Vote." *Commonweal*, 21 November 1980, pp. 650-51.

Fairbanks, James David. "The Evangelical Right: Beginnings of Another Symbolic Crusade." Paper presented to the American Political Science Association, New York, 5 September 1981.

Guth, James L. "The Politics of the Evangelical Right: An Interpretive Essay." Paper presented to the American Political Science Association, New York, 5 September 1981.

——————————. "The Southern Baptist Clergy: Vanguard of the Evangelical Right?" Paper presented to the Southern Political Science Association, Memphis, 6 November 1981.

Lipset, Seymour Martin and Raab, Earl. "The Election and the Evangelicals." *Commentary*, March 1981, pp. 25-31.

Mouw, Richard. "Assessing the Moral Majority." *Reformed Journal*, June 1981, pp. 13-15.

Smedes, Lewis B. "Cleaning Up the Nation: Nine Theses on Politics and Morality." *Reformed Journal*, June 1980, pp. 10-13.

"What's Wrong with Born-Again Politics? A Symposium." *Christian Century*, 22 October 1980, pp. 1002-4.

Zwier, Robert and Smith, Richard. "Christian Politics and the New Right." *Christian Century*, 8 October 1980, pp. 937-41.